TABLE OF CONTENTS

Page

ACRONYMS

COE	Contemporary Operational Environment
FM	Field Manual
IRA	Irish Republican Army
IPB	Intelligence Preparation of the Battlefield
JP	Joint Publication
KLA	Liberation Army
KKK	Ku Klux Klan
METT-TC	Mission, Enemy, Terrain, Troops, Technology, and Civil
SAMS	School of Advanced Military Studies
UN	United Nations
US	United States

CHAPTER 1

INTRODUCTION

> If you know the enemy and know yourself, you need not
> fear the result of a hundred battles. If you know yourself but not
> the enemy, for every victory gained you will also suffer a defeat.

> Sun Tzu, *The Art of War*

Today's contemporary operational environment is filled with a multiplicity of

threats that endanger the security and interests of America. More than ever they are

harder to anticipate and more difficult to combat. A growing number of borderless threats

complicate the strategic environment, making its challenges less predictable. These

threats include trans-national terrorism and those that use extremist religious ideologies

to export it. This is most challenging problem for planners at all levels, including military

planners.

The United States (US) military is operating in 120 countries all over the world.

Many individuals and groups within those countries share beliefs and ideologies quite

different from those in the US. In particular, groups within countries, such as Iraq, Sudan,

Kosovo, Afghanistan, Congo, and others, have beliefs and religious ideologies that are

quite different than those of the majority of the US population. There are even factions

within each of those countries that hold ideas that are different from the orthodox

teaching of their own religion. Nevertheless, for various reasons, it remains in the

national security interests of the US to continue to have some level of bilateral

relationship with such countries. However, at times those beliefs coupled with corruption

and crime have become points of contention and have been the impetus for national and international conflict. This study is not intended to be a study about religion in itself; rather it seeks to analyze aspects of extremist religious ideologies.

The perceived problem is military planners are not doing a thorough job analyzing the extremist religious ideology of threat or enemy combatants within the contemporary operating environment, yet they are developing strategies and issuing orders that should entail information about their ideology.

The primary question this research seeks to answer is: Do Army planners at the operational and tactical levels account for extremist religious ideologies in the formulation of military strategy? Secondary questions include the following:

1. What must planners consider in relation to extremist religious ideologies?

2. What are the implications of not accounting for religious ideologies in strategy development?

3. What is the current military doctrine relating to the subject?

The major constraint in conducting this research is this author's ability to empathize with those who hold and support religious ideologies that serve to breed and support extremist behaviors. However, an adequate understanding of many of the intricacies of the extremist religious ideologies covered in this research was derived through a careful examination of key phrases and historical events.

Although many terms were examined while conducting this research, the key terms are "ideology," "extremist religious ideology," " terrorist," and "strategy." Definitions of ideology, extremist religious ideology, and terrorist are:

Ideology: An ideology is a collection of ideas. According to one definition the actual word ideology is attributed to Count Destutt de Tracy as he used the word in the eighteenth century to mean "a science of ideas." [1] Additionally, the definition suggests that an ideology includes philosophical tendencies or a set of ideas proposed by the dominate class of society to all members of this society. [2] Ideology embraces politicized religion that uses it to perpetuate prejudice. It also creates a symbolic structure of social life. [3]

Extremist Religious Ideology: Individuals or groups who use religious principles to support the conduct of mental or physical harm to individuals or cause harm or terrorist actions towards others. Examples of groups with extremist religious ideologies are listed below.

Army for the Liberation of Rwanda: The Army for the Liberation of Rwanda better known as the Former Armed Forces, was the army of the Rwandan Hutu regime that carried out the genocide of 500,000 or more Tutsis and regime opponents in 1994. The Interahamwe was the civilian militia force that carried out much of the killing. The groups merged after they were forced from Rwanda into the Democratic Republic of the Congo in 1994. The group seeks to topple Rwanda's Tutsi-dominate government and reinstitute Hutu Control. Area of Operation: Mostly Democratic Republic of the Congo and Rwanda, but a few may operate in Burundi [4]

Croatian Democratic Union (Croation: Hrvatska Demokratska Zajednica): The right-wing Christian Democratic Party was founded in June 1989. It led Croatia to independence in 1991. The extremist wing of Hrvatska Demokratska Zajednica have been responsible for a number of bomb attacks. [5]

Terrorist: One who engages in the act of terrorism. One who systematically uses act of terror as a means of coercion. [6]

Defining "strategy" is a little more complicated. This is because the term has multiple definitions and the focus strategy tends to have slightly different perspectives at each level of war.

From a historical prospective, the term strategy is taken from the Greek word "strategos" which means "the art of the general."[7] The term originally denoted the function of military planning for battles. Carl von Clausewitz stated that "All men can see the tactics whereby I conquer, but what none can see is the strategy out of which victory is evolved."[8] This suggests that tactics is the art of using troops in battle and strategy is the art of using battles to win the war. He further seems to clearly express strategy as something occurring at the operational level of war and that it is associated with winning campaigns. However, in his definition of tactics, he does not specifically say that commanders at the tactical use strategy in their effort to win battles.

Today, many people tend to only associate strategy with the national military strategy objective which is essentially the same as the National Military Strategy. Some even go a step further and associate strategy with combatant commanders, which is essentially theater strategy. Few are insightful enough to insist that strategy is also found at the operational and tactical levels of war. Understanding strategy at the operational level is clear because it is outlined in many of the various definitions of strategy. One definition is found in FM 3-0, which states that strategy is the art and science of developing and employing armed forces and other instruments of national power in a synchronized fashion to secure national or multinational objectives.[9] This definition tends to support operational level strategy because FM 3-0 provides doctrine for operational level commanders.

4

Next, what is tactical level strategy? Tactical level strategy is not necessarily a doctrinal term but commanders at all levels develop and use strategy in conducting military operation. To understand strategy at this level, one must look at strategy in its simplest form, that is, strategy is planning that involves some type of decision making process that produces courses of action that gives the commander advantage when facing the enemy. At the tactical level commanders are required to implement fundamental concepts such as the principles of war, tenents of battle and the basic elements of operational design when engaging in battle. The commander must also know how and when to use defensive and offensive strategies such as flank, encirclement, penetration, feint, and others when developing plans for and conducting operations. It should be clear that commanders at all levels are involved in making and implementing strategy. One writer stated, "Each level is concerned with planning (making strategy), which involves analyzing the situation, estimating friendly and enemy capabilities and limitations, and devising possible courses of action."[10] Another writer perhaps summed it up well as he stated the following:

> Indeed, in the 20th century, tactics have been termed operational strategy. Strategy is limited by what tactics are possible; given the size, training, and morale of forces, type and number of weapons available, terrain, weather, and quality and location of enemy forces, the tactics to be used are dependent on strategic considerations. Strategist (planners) at all levels must carefully assess the security environment and consider things such as friendly forces, enemy forces, vulnerabilities, threats, challenges and opportunities.[11]

Now, in order to produce relevancy for this research, it is assumed that the US military will conduct operations in the future in regions that will have militant and extremist religious factions which may threaten the peace and security of US allies or will create problems that are in opposition to US interests. It is assumed that these religious

5

factions will continue to conduct non-conventional warfare against US military personnel and their allies. It is further assumed that US military planners will be responsible for planning operations for nation-states that in which military operations are not currently being executed. This study will help current and future military planners as they develop military strategies for military operations in those areas.

Finally, an analysis of significant aspects of the operational environment of the US during the Pre- and Post-Civil period and in Northern Ireland, Korea, Kosovo, and Somalia are presented. An analysis of extremist religious factions and groups within these countries is used to help set the basis for answering the thesis and the secondary questions.

Again, the primary question that this research seeks to answer is: Do Army planners at the operational and tactical levels account for extremist religious ideologies in the formulation of military strategy?

---

[1]Edmund F. Byrne, Mission in Modern Life: A Public Role for Religious Beliefs; available from http://www.bu.edu/wcp/Papers/Poli/PoliByrn.htm; Internet; accessed on 20 September 2005.

[2]Ibid.

[3]Ibid.

[4]Sean D. Hill, *Extremist Groups: An International Compilation of Terrorist Organizations, Violent Political Groups, and Issue-Oriented Militant Movements* (Huntsville, TX, Office of International Criminal Justice and the Instituted for the Study of Violent Groups, Sam Houston State University, 2002), 93.

[5]Ibid., 335.

[6]*Webster's Ninth New Collegiate Dictionary* (Spring Field, MA: Merriam-Webster, Inc., 1990), 1218

[7]*Merriam-Webster Dictionary* [dictionary on-line]; available from http://www.m-w.com/cgi-bin/dictionary?book=Dictionary&va=strategy; Internet; accessed on 16 May 2006.

[8]Sun Tzu, *The Art of War* [book on-line]; available from http://classics.mit.edu/Tzu/artwar.html; Internet; accessed on 16 May 2006.

[9]Headquarters, Department of the Army, FM 3-0, *Operations* (Washington, DC: GPO, 2001), 2-4.

[10]"Three Levels of War" [article on-line]; available from http://www.cadre.maxwell.af.mil/ar/MENTOR/vol1/sec02.pdf#search='%E2%80%9CEach%20level%20is%20concerned%20with%20planning%20%28making%20strategy%29%2C; Internet; accessed on 23 March 2006.

[11]The Molossian Military Academy, Homepage; available from http://www.molossia.org/milacademy/strategy.html; Internet; accessed on 23 March 2006.

CHAPTER 2

LITERATURE REVIEW

There are many books and other writings that address the issue of extremist religious ideologies; however, very few link military strategy with radical or extremist religious ideology. Nevertheless, this author's task is to link the two themes together in order to answer the thesis question. Below is an examination some of the books and periodicals used in conducting this research.

Books

Books used in this research include: *Islam, Fundamentalism, and the Betrayal of Tradition* by Joseph Lumbard; *The Receding Shadow of the Prophet: The Rise and Fall of Radical Political Islam* by Nikolas K. Gvosdev and Ray Takeyh; *The Islamic Threat: Myth or Reality* by John L. Esposito; *The Terrorism Almanac* by James L. Outman and Lisa M. Outman; *Unmasking Terror: A Global Review of Terrorist Activities* by Glenn E. Howard, and *Memories of Bosnia*, by Ronald Cobb. Additionally, articles by Umej Bhatia, "In the Shade of Death: A Critical Reading on Sayyid QutB's Qur'anic Exegesis," and several leading newspapers and periodicals were used in this research.

The book *Survey of International Terrorism* describes how the followers of various religious ideologies take extreme measure to defend and support the teaching of their leaders. The book includes the ideological problem between the Roman Catholics, Anglicans, and Protestants in Northern Ireland. The author goes in-depth to explain that the dispute fueled the extremist actions of groups such as the IRA, the Loyalist Volunteer Force, and the Real IRA in Northern Ireland.

In his book *Islam, Fundamentalism, and the Betrayal of Tradition*, Joseph E. B. Lumbard describes the Islamic tradition and how many followers have abandoned the traditional teachings. Perhaps the following quote from the book best describes the context of the book, "We are thus faced with a predicament wherein the religion that has nurtured some of us for our entire lives, and some of us, since we embraced Islam, has come to be identified for many of our neighbors and co-workers with the ideologies of a deviant if not heretical minority."[1] The author goes on to present authentic Islamic faith, radical supporters, and beliefs that are inconsistent with the Koran.

The Receding Shadow of the Prophet: The Rise and Fall of Radical Political Islam explores how Islam plays a vital role in the politics of the Middle East and how Islamic revolutionaries are able to spark mass uprisings including acts of radical idealism and acts of terrorism. Grosdev and Takeyh go on to examine how the Islamic movement gained strongholds in the Balkans, Egypt, and Algeria. One quote from *The Receding Shadow of the Prophet: The Rise and Fall of Radical Political Islam* that captures the essence of the book is: "Islamism is an ideology of wrath that is capable of mobilizing the masses, but it provides little guidance for actual governance."[2]

Within the pages of the *Terrorism Almanac*, the reader will find a description of religious terrorism acts that have occurred in earlier and modern times. This includes chapters on how the Roman Catholic Church through the Spanish Inquisition of the fifteenth century punished people who were considered enemies of Christianity--specifically Jews and Muslims, but also Christians who had beliefs different from those held by the Church. It further talks about how Islam has become the religion in the twentieth century most often associated with terrorism.

James L. Outman and Lisa M. Outman go on to point out that they believe that in modern times, religious terrorism has been more violent and deadlier than before. They say that terrorist who believe that they are acting on instructions from God often have such confidence in the rightness of their cause that they will have less hesitation about killing large numbers of civilians.[3] Outman and Outman further point out that the Muslim world is upset with the West because of western ideas and the widespread poverty gap. Additionally, the Muslim clerics and religious leaders are teaching their followers not to adopt western ideas and values but to observe only their religious teachings in order to remove western influences from their society. This has lead followers to view violent terrorists as evidence of religious piety (devotion), self-sacrifice (for example, by carrying out a suicide bombing) and praise as a way to get to paradise.[4]

An essay by Umej Bhatia entitled, "In the Shade of Death: A Critical Reading of Sayyid Qutb's Quranic Exegesis," captures an important statement that shows how the words of a prominent figure can use a religious authority to spur the actions of his followers. Specifically, Bhatia notes that Qutb's writing influenced the actions of people such as the Ayatollah Komeini and Usama bin Laden. He states that his Sunni fundamentalism writing has impacted modern Shite fundamentalism. He further states that Mohammed Qutb, Sayyid's brother, continued to proclaim the message of Sayyid's message to the Sunni world, including Saudi Arabia and Muslim Brotherhood (Wahhabism). He points out that Qutb's writing is simply an ideologically charged interpretation of the Quran written to generate Muslim interest and action.[5]

Glenn Howard's book entitled, *Unmasking Terror: A Global Review of Terrorist Activities* also describes aspects of Sayyid Qutb's writing. The subsection listed below shows the tone and feelings of Qutb.

In the subsection "The Application of Vehemence" subtitled "The Policy of Paying the Price," Abu Bakr Naji warns against the dangers of anything other than maximum violence as a deterrent, or as a response, even if the response should take years. The response, the author states, "is best done by other groups and in other countries than those suffering the act of enmity . . . to give the enemy the sense of being surrounded and his interests exposed . . . and to confuse him." An example of this method would be in response to the Egyptians' imprisonment of mujahideen, an attack by mujahideen upon an Egyptian embassy in the Arabian Peninsula or the Maghreb, or the kidnapping of Egyptian diplomats, who should be "liquidated horrifically" if the mujahideen's demands are not met.[6]

The final book, *Memories of Bosnia,* by Ronald Lee Cobb, describes the 35th Division's SFOR 13 NATO Peacekeeping Mission in Bosnia. The following quote from the author summarizes the focus of the book.

> Knowing the culture and religion of the indigenous people in a nation is fundamental to Information Operations work because of the many powerful emotional issues that are linked to the local, social values. These emotional issues are part and parcel of the culture and of the religion. If they are overlooked it can hinder the fulfillment of the military mission. The history of the United States military operation s of all branches shows that too often culture, religion, and the ensuing emotional issues have indeed often been neglected to the peril of mission accomplishment.[7]

This book captures the essence of the thesis. The author seems to validate the importance of military planners understanding the religion and culture of indigenous people. He believes to understand the religious thoughts and motivations of people are an important element in accomplishing military missions.

News Papers and Periodicals

Articles from leading newspapers and periodicals, such as *USA Today, The Christian Science Monitor, India Today, Economist,* and the RAND Corporation, are used in this research. Some of the abstracts are listed below.

> For the first time since the end of the Cold War, the US finds itself in an intense competition for hearts and minds. This time, it is competing against radical Islamic fundamentalists for the support of the Muslim World. Here, Cohen discusses the necessity for the US government and its allies to combat militant Islamist ideology that seeks its downfall and the demise of its core values.[8]

> Indonesia has been beset by a surge of Islamist radicalism and terrorism from militant groups such as Jemaah Islamiyah, responsible for the October 2002 nightclub bombing in Bali, among other attacks. Though the sprouting of these extremist cells is troubling, it is not yet translating into support at the polls for the religious radicalism that would move Indonesia away from the world's mainstream and ally it with the least- developed nations of Islam.[9]

> A majority of over 11,000 informal madarsas in Pakistan cater to the poorer segment and offer education in the Quran, Hadith (sayings of the Prophet) and Arabic, the so-called Dars-e-Nizamia curriculum. Some have introduced computer literacy, but math, history, geography and English are not taught. Run by factional religious groups controlling mosques, they are accused of promoting sectarian thought. An example is the Darul Quran, a seminary and mosque in Faisalabad that claims to have 4,200 students from Pakistan as well as from Sudan, Philippines, Afghanistan and Central Asian states.[10]

> A few short weeks ago, Saudi Arabia looked well on the road to recovery from the public-relations disaster of September 11, 2001. But the kingdom's darker side has a way of emerging to cast shadows over the brightest hopes. This week a Saudi court condemned three prominent liberals to serve between six and nine years behind bars. The three men, a poet and two professors, were among 13 intellectuals arrested in March last year, shortly after calling publicly for Saudi Arabia to evolve into a constitutional monarchy. Among the three men's "crimes" cited by the judges were their description of the kingdom's educational system and Wahhabi religious ideology as causes of extremism.[11]

In light of 9/11 and the war on terrorism, it is important for U.S. leaders to develop a shaping strategy toward the Muslim world. This study describes a framework to identify major ideological orientations within Islam, examines critical cleavages between Muslim groups, and traces the long-term and immediate causes of Islamic radicalism. It also outlines political and military strategies available to help ameliorate conditions that produce extremism.[12]

These articles show some of the mechanisms through which radical Islamism is being taught to people in the Muslim world. These extremist principles are causing many to move away from western ideas and to embrace radical fundamentalist teachings. Each tends to point out the realism of the threat that extremist religious ideologies present to the US, US Allies, and any other nations.

---

[1]Joseph E. B. Lumbard, *Islam, Fundamentalism, and the Betrayal of Tradition* (Canada: World Wisdom, Inc., 2004), 16.

[2]Nikolas K. Gvosdev and Ray Takeyh, *The Receding Shadow of the Prophet: The Rise and Fall of Radical Political Islam* (Westport, CT: Greenwood Publishing Group, Inc., 2004), 16.

[3]James L. Outman and Lisa M. Outman, *Terrorism Almanac* (New York: Thomson Gale Publishers, 2003), 187.

[4]Ibid.

[5]Umej Bhatia, "In the Shade of Death: A Critical Reading on Sayyid QutB's Qur'anic Exegesis" [article on-line]; available from http://www.fsu.edu/~proghum/interculture/In%20the%20Shade%20of%20Death.htm; Internet; accessed on 30 November 2005.

[6]Glenn E. Howard, *Unmasking Terror: A Global Review of Terrorist Activities* (Washington, DC: Brookings Institute and the Jamestown Foundation, 2005), 596 [book on-line]; available from http://brookings.edu/unmaskingterror; Internet; accessed on 3 January 2006.

[7]Ronald Lee Cobb, *Memories of Bosnia* (Bloomington, IN: AuthorHouse Publishers, 2004).

[8]"Are Islamist Schools a Threat to U.S.?" *USA Today* 133, no. 2715 (December 2004): 6.

[9]John Hughes, "Turbulent Indonesia, Moderate Islam," *Christian Science Monitor* (14 April 2004): 9.

[10]Hasan Zaidi, "Over to the General; Monitoring Madarsas-Potential Breeding Grounds for Extremism-is as Serious a Challenge for Musharraf as Reining in Militants," *India Today* (1 August 2005): 58.

[11]"International: The Suffocating Limits of Reform; Saudi Arabia London," *The Economist* 375, no. 8427 (21 May 2005): 65.

[12]Angel M. Rabasa, Cheryl Benard, Peter Chalk, C. Christine Fair, Theodore Karasik, Rollie Lal, Ian Lesser, and David Thaler, *The Muslim World After 9-11* (Santa Monica, CA: RAND Corporation, 2004); available from http://www.rand.org/ publications/RB/RB151/; Internet; accessed on 20 November 2005.

CHAPTER 3

RESEARCH METHODOLOGY

The methodology used to conduct research for this the paper was predominantly firsthand (interviews) and secondary research. All information was carefully analyzed for validity and accuracy.

The firsthand information was gathered from officers with experience or firsthand knowledge about various extremist religious ideologies, especially those that are in the current contemporary operational environment. This collection method included surveys from future planners in the School of Advanced Military Studies (SAMS) and other officers who are currently attending the Command and General Staff College. The guidelines for the interviews and surveys were set by the thesis committee and author. Research questions used during the interviews included the following:

1. Should military planners at the operational and tactical levels consider the extremist religious ideology of the enemy when developing strategy for military plans?

2. Should information about extremist religious ideology be included in operation orders?

3. What is the utility, if any, of knowing information about the enemy's extremist religious ideology?

4. Have you ever received information about the extremist religious ideology of an enemy or opposing force from a military planner for any operation you have participated in? Was the information adequate enough? Explain. (Please identify: Exercise or Real-world)

5. When developing a strategy for an operation, what considerations, if any, should you as an operational/tactical level planner give to the possibility of the enemy having an extremist religious ideology? (Please identify: Exercise or Real-world)

6. What military doctrinal provision directs (or suggests) military planners to gather, analyze, and disseminate information about extremist religious ideologies when developing strategies for an operation?

7. Knowing what you know now about extremist religious ideology, if you had to develop a strategy for an operational or tactical level operation, how would you account for the possibility of an extremist religious ideology?

The secondary information used in this research was gathered using various methods and sources. This included obtaining research materials from the Combined Armed Research Library, the internet, documents and books.

Additionally, the secondary research information presented in chapter 4 about the nature and actions of individual and groups that had or supported an extremist religious ideology were presented was evaluated against the stated definitions of the terms ideology, extremist religious ideology, and terrorist.

CHAPTER 4

ANALYTICAL VIEW OF CASE STUDIES OF INDIVIDUALS AND FACTIONS HAVING EXTREMIST RELIGIOUS IDEOLOGIES

> Studying the past has a way of introducing humility--a first stage toward gaining detachment--because it suggests the continuity of the problems we confront and the unoriginality of most of our solutions for them. It is a good way of putting things in perspective, of stepping back to take a wider view.
>
> John Lewis Gaddis

Introduction

There are literally hundreds of factions in various countries all over the world that support or have religious ideologies that are considered extreme. They are extreme because they conduct or sponsor violent acts, and they seek to undermine the legitimacy of a nation's government while instilling fear in the hearts and minds of the population. These factions or groups have often used a distorted view of religion to propagate their agenda. At the top of the agenda for some and one of the greatest concerns for America is trans-national terrorism and those that use extremist religious ideologies to export it. It is important for military planners to know why extremist religious ideologies exist and why the ideology behind the threat resonates among its supporters. However, the problem is one that has already saturated the contemporary operational environment. Military planners must consider every implication pertaining to extremist ideologies, including extremist religious ideologies in order to develop better strategies that enable successful operations with the contemporary operational environment.

This chapter presents five different historical case studies and concludes with list of considerations and implications taken from the study that are important and valuable to

17

today's military planners. The case studies include the pre-Civil War and post reconstruction US, Northern Ireland, Korea, Kosovo and Somalia (Horn of Africa).

Extremist Religious Ideology in America (Pre-Civil War and Post-Civil War)

This case study is relevant to the study of extremist religious ideology and military strategy because the military was one of the primary instruments of national power used to help resolve many of the extremist problems that occurred during the period of pre and post-reconstruction. It is well known that Colonel Robert E. Lee led a detachment of federal forces to suppress John Brown's anti-slavery uprising at Harpers Ferry, Virginia. Additionally, during reconstruction President Ulysses S. Grant often directed federal troops to the south to enforce the provision of the fifteenth amendment. This amendment guaranteed the rights of citizens of the US to vote shall not be denied or abridged by the US or any State on account of race, color, or previous condition of servitude.[1] There are many accounts of when the President specifically ordered federal troops to enforce the Fifteenth Amendment Enforcement Act of 1871 better known as the "The Ku Klux Klan (KKK) Act." This Act specifically served to protect black suffrage and targeted the violent activities of the KKK and other groups. This case study serves to remind military planners that it is quite conceivable that the military will be called upon to deal with similar domestic problems as they occur today.

Extremist Religious Leaders

The idea of groups using religion as a vehicle to further the extremist ideology of the group or organization is not a new phenomenon nor is it something that has not plagued the US before. There are many recorded examples of how religious leaders in both the Northern and Southern US taught biblical lessons and preached sermons that served as an impetus to further their cause of their followers. Some religious leaders performed actions and preached sermons that caused others to commit acts of terror-- physical and mental--and even acts of murder against to those that opposed their views. Examples from the north included the Reverend Henry Beecher and John Brown. And from the south there were religious leaders like Bishop James Mead and William J. Simmons of the KKK. Arguably all of them, including the KKK, are considered supporters of or individuals that propagated an extremist religious ideology.

The Reverend Henry Beecher was a Congregationalist Minister who opposed the Fugitive Slave Law. His actions were significant because it is believed that he was personally responsible for furnishing abolitionists rifles so they could physically fight against the federal law. Although some supported the actions of Beecher, his actions clearly sent the message to his supporters and others to take physical actions against those that supported the Fugitive Slave Laws. Those actions included engaging in armed conflict which resulted in the death of some followers and supporters.

John Brown, although not officially given the title Reverend, was known as a preacher and abolitionist that was very outspoken and influential. He is a significant figure in this study because it is believed that he led a group of men on an attack against a proslavery group of men in Pottawatomie, Kansas. His group, which included his four sons, reportedly dragged five proslavery men from their homes and hacked them to death. Although it is undetermined whether or not Brown actually killed the proslavery supporters, it is clear that his actions encouraged the extremist action of his followers, including his own children.

Although the north had its share of problematic religious leaders, many southern religious leaders also abused their positions. Among many things, they played a significant part in helping to maintain an ethnic suppressive culture that became an everyday part of the fabric of southern Antebellum life. In a paper entitled, "Ol' Satan's Church is Here Below Southern Religion and Black Slavery in the Antebellum South," Leif E. Trondsen argues that many American preachers in the south did not teach or preach a Biblical Theology that was grounded in the Christian faith, rather they proclaimed a type of mind control that served to further the cause of the south. Trondsen said that the southern teaching was different than that of the historical Christian Faith, as practiced in Europe and elsewhere for nearly two millennia.[2] He states, "Southern religion was an ad hoc and artificial creation, the principal goal of which was to prop up the increasingly struggling institution of Southern slavery. Above all, it was an ideological tool for black repression. As such, Southern religion was fraught with glaring theological and moral contradictions."[3] In his essay he cited an example of a sermon given by Bishop James Mead of Virginia in 1856:

> Having thus shown you the chief duties you owe to your great Master in heaven, I now come to lay before you the duties you owe to your masters and mistresses on earth. And for this you have one general rule that you ought always to carry in your minds; and that is to do all service for them as if you did it for God himself.

> Poor creatures! You little consider, when you are idle and neglectful of your master's business, when you steal, and waste, and hurt any of their substance, when your are saucy and impudent, when you are telling them lies and deceiving them, or when you prove stubborn and sullen, and will not do the work your are set about without stripes and vexation--you do not consider, I say, that what faults you are guilty of towards your masters and mistresses are faults against God himself, who hath set your masters and mistresses over you in his stead, and expects that you would do for them just as you would do for him. And pray do not think that I want to deceive you when I tell you that your masters and mistresses

are God's overseers, and that, if you are faulty towards them, God himself will punish you severely for it in the next world.[4]

The problem with this sermon is the religious leader purposefully preached words using religious principles to support a personal or societal agenda. Arguably, the intent of the religious leader was to keep the subjects in bondage by saying that God was aligned with the masters and mistresses, and the slaves' disobediences would displease God, thus putting them in jeopardy of receiving punishment from God then and in the future. Since many of the subjects could not read or write, the religious leader's words were authoritative, despite the fact that many of them brainwashed the subjects and caused mental harm because they purposefully distorted the truth in their sermons. Another example of this outlined by Trondsen was a distorted teaching of a passage of scripture taken from the Biblical Book of Ephesians:

> Servants, be obedient to them that are your masters according to the flesh, with fear and trembling, in singleness of your heart, as unto Christ; Not with eye-service, as men pleasers; but as servants of Christ, doing the will of God from the heart; With good will doing service, as to the Lord, and not to men: Knowing that whatsoever good thing any man doeth, the same shall he receive of the Lord, whether he be bond or free.[5]

According to Trodsen, this passage was frequently used to keep the subjects under subjection to those that oppressed them.[6] Again, the problem with this is the religious leader wanted to maintain an environment that kept subjects submissive and for them to fear their masters and mistresses in the same manner they reverenced God. Actions like these continued throughout the Pre-Civil War period.

Shortly after the civil war and during Reconstruction, the KKK emerged as a splinter group from the defeated Confederate Army claiming superiority over certain groups of southern civilians, Union military veterans and various ethnic groups. This group often used people claiming to be ministers, evangelists, and pastors to further their cause.

The goal of the Klan was to create an environment that undermined the federal government and the new reconstruction laws. The group was bent on continuing the traditions that were in place under the Confederacy. To do this, the members of the group would conduct acts of terror to cause southern whites and ex-slaves from supporting new laws and from banding together to make a strong, united front that could oppose the Klan. The Klan even infiltrated and influenced the southern elected officials to support the passing of segregation laws and a federal act to prevent the federal government from using the military to monitor voting stations and other governmental actions.[7] After some initial success, the group ceased to be the force it was immediately after reconstruction.

In the early 1920s, the KKK again emerged as a group that threatened the safety and security of the many within the US. This time the group was led by a former Methodist preacher, William J. Simmons.[8] The new Klan was organized in Stone Mountain, Georgia, as a patriotic, Protestant fraternal society. However, the KKK continued to promote race supremacy, religious extremism, and a general hatred of various ethnic groups within the US and world wide. They also denounced those that supported or had close relationships with those groups. According to one account, the victims were usually blacks, Jews, Roman Catholics, Mexicans and various immigrants, sometimes, however, they were white, Protestant, and female. Klansmen attacked people they considered "immoral" or "traitors" to the white race.[9] The same source noted an incident in which ladies in Alabama and Georgia were flogged by ministers that supported the KKK.

In Alabama, . . . a divorcee with two children was flogged for the crime of remarrying, and then given a jar of Vaseline for her wounds. In Georgia a woman was given 60 lashes for a vague charge of "immorality and failure to go to church." And when her 15-year-old son ran to her rescue, he received the same treatment. In both cases the leaders of the Klansmen responsible turned out to be ministers.[10]

The Klan not only used religion but they used some religious leaders to help further their act of terrorism. They also used the power and influence of the organization to influence local and state governments.[11] The next section outlines planning considerations and implications derived from this case study.

Planning Considerations

From this case study planners must consider the following in relation to extremist religious ideologies.

1. People who propagate extremist religious ideologies tend to exert tremendous control over their followers.

2. The power and impact of spoken words. Often times the religious extremists words and actions can cause people to commit acts of violence and even murder. John Brown's fiery words and actions caused some of his followers, including his sons, to have reportedly murdered proslavery conformist.

3. Extremist religious ideological beliefs are often times rooted deeply in culture and tradition. The KKK were opposed to change and would take extreme measures to protect their common belief and to propagate it by all available means, including using fear tactics and even murder.

4. Extremist religious ideology is often times associated with hate crimes, both passive and overt. The KKK used religion as a front while they taught and preached messages of hate.

5. The extent of influence held by leaders who propagate an extremist religious ideology. Often times the influence affects social, political, and economic realms.

Planning Implications

From this case study, planners should consider the implications of not accounting for religious ideologies in strategy development.

1. Military planners will be forced to conduct crisis action planning instead of deliberate planning.

2. Planners could miss the chance to gain support from the populace. Often times there are segments of the population that do not support the extremist religious ideology but they are force to because of their proximity to family and friends or some other interest. This segment could become a support base if they feel they can be protected and that the people or forces that are propagating the extremist ideology will be defeated in a timely manner.

3. Planners could miss the chance to introduce a viable information operation campaign. Often times there are vulnerable in the messages that are spoken by those to spread extremist ideologies. The planner should be ready to institute a campaign that discredits the extremist ideology. As mentioned earlier in the paper, many extremist teach a doctrine that is different than the original orthodox teachings of their religion.

4. Planners could miss the opportunity to gain valuable intelligence. The planner must start gathering information about the extremist ideology early. Creditable Human

Intelligence help the planner understand how the extremist ideology will affect military operations in the area of operations.

5. Planners could fail to understand the magnitude of the problem. Often times the extremist religious ideology is so infectious that it serves to unite people. The extremist tends to develop an interwoven support system in which supporters are in key positions in government, community, banking, and industry.

Extremist Religious Ideology in Northern Ireland

This case study is relevant to the study of extremist religious ideology and military strategy because it is an ongoing British military operation that has presented some important lessons learned that can benefit military planners in the development of plans for possible military operations in a similar operational environment. These lessons learned can serve to assist the military planner in developing plans to target, neutralize, or isolate religious extremist religious leaders or organizations.

The Extremist Religious Ideology

The major religious groups in Northern Ireland are the Roman Catholics, Anglicans and the Protestants. Although all subscribe to the Christianity, the fundamental teaching of their faith does not condone criminal acts, followers and splinter groups from each have planned, committed, and supported extremist acts of violence.

The troubles and tensions in Northern Ireland between these groups have been longstanding for over three-hundred years. The most notable event occurred on 12 July 1690 when forces of the Anglican English King, William of Orange defeated King James II, the Roman Catholic King, at the Battle of the Boyne, which gave the Protestants supremacy in Ireland.[12] Then in the year 1796, the Protestants established an annual

Orange Parade that celebrated their victory. The march is normally led by a group that

calls themselves the Apprentice Boys who are named after a group of young apprentices

that bided "No Surrender" as they held the gates of Derry in 1689 against the forces of

King James.[13] This annual parade by the Protestants in the predominately Roman

Catholic neighborhoods is a point of tension and violent clashes between the two groups.

Although in recent years, the two parties have attempted to resolve their

differences and establish a peaceful society, the results of their agreements and actions

have not lasted. It is estimated that between 1968 and 1994, over 3,500 people died and

over 35,000 were injured in Northern Ireland as a direct result of the fighting.[14]

Additionally, Northern Ireland has been plagued by robberies, bombings, assassinations,

and other acts of terrorism. Throughout the years, the civil rights of individuals in

Northern Ireland have been seriously eroded, and freedom in the name of safety has been

sacrificed to some.

One splinter group of the Protestants called the Loyalists has taken responsibility

for many acts of terrorism against the Roman Catholics. Those acts of terrorism include

the following:

> The UVF's [Ulster Volunteer Force's] 1966 shooting of four Roman
> Catholics, one fatally, outside a Belfast pub. This attack was the first major act of
> sectarian violence since Ireland was divided, and it spurred Roman Catholic
> activism, which soon turned violent.
> The UVF's [Ulster Volunteer Force's] 1969 bombing of a power station
> near Belfast. Initially attributed to the IRA, this attack also helped trigger the
> Troubles.
> The UVF's [Ulster Volunteer Force 's] 1971 bombing of a Belfast pub,
> which killed 15 people.

A pair of UVF [Ulster Volunteer Force] bombings in Dublin and Monaghan, both in the Republic of Ireland, on May 17, 1974, that killed 33 civilians, making this day the deadliest of the conflict.

The UDA's [Ulster Defense Association's] October 1993 machine-gun attack on a bar in the Northern Ireland town of Greysteel, which killed eight civilians.

The LVF [Loyalist Volunteer Force] killing of Sinn Fein leader Gerry Adams' nephew in January 1998.

A fierce campaign of intimidation and abuse of Roman Catholic schoolgirls in Belfast between June and October 2001.[15]

A splinter group from the Roman Catholic Irish Republican Army (IRA) calling themselves the Real IRA have also claimed responsibility for several acts of violent acts against the Protestants. It is reported that in August 1998, the Real IRA detonated a five-hundred-pound car bomb in the Irish town of Omagh, killing twenty-nine people, including a woman eight months pregnant with twins.[16] The Real IRA has also been linked to almost thirty attacks in Northern Ireland and six in London, including a failed attempt to blow up a bridge over the Thames River and minor explosions at British Broadcasting Corporation Television and MI6 intelligence headquarters.[17] The next section outlines planning considerations and implications derived from this case study.

Planning Considerations

From this case study, planners should consider the following planning considerations in relation to extremist religious ideologies when developing strategies for military operations.

1. Normally, the extremist religious ideology is historical and is again deeply rooted in the culture.

2. Oftentimes extremist rebels who cloak themselves with a religious ideology will fight for ideals such as pride, honor, and recognition. As with the conflict in

Northern Ireland, religious factions or groups could fight for centuries and many lives could be lost, without reaching a true peaceful solution. At end state, the final result could still be an environment plagued with people and splinter groups that conduct robberies, bombings, assassinations, and other acts of terrorism.

3. Individuals or groups that support extremist religious ideologies often times conduct robberies, bombings, assassinations, and other acts of terrorism. Factions in Northern Ireland, such as the Real IRA have been linked to almost thirty attacks in Northern Ireland and other attacks in London. In each attack innocent people were killed or injured.

4. Kinetic targeting methods may be ineffective or obsolete. New targeting methods must be developed to target, isolate or neutralize the person or group with the extremist religious ideology and may have to be replaced with non-kinetic or passive targeting methods. The ongoing operations in Northern Ireland by the British military operation has provided many important lessons learned that can benefit military planners in developing plans to target, neutralize, or isolate religious extremist religious leaders or organizations. Three lessons learned, two operational and one tactical, are listed below. Particular attention should be given to intelligence gathering.

> Operational Lesson 1: Existing British military doctrine was inappropriate for operating in Northern Ireland. Despite having extensive experience in counter-terrorist operations in Kenya, Malaya, Aden, Hong Kong, Cyprus, and many other colonial outposts, the British Army could not apply proven approaches and methods due to the unique status of Northern Ireland as part of the United Kingdom. For example, the traditional approach to suppressing riots involved the following steps: (1) British soldiers would form into a tightly knit box formation, (2) deploy barbed wire to separate themselves from the unruly crowd, (3) order the crowd to disperse or they would be fired upon, and (4) shoot a few of the obvious ringleaders in the hostile crowd. Shooting down UK citizens (under the watchful eye of TV) was understood by military leaders to be a "no go" from the

28

beginning. (A wise decision in view of the furor caused when the 1st Parachute Regiment shot 13 demonstrators on what came to be called "Bloody Sunday." The British military also had to abandon traditional, doctrinally prescribed, intelligence-gathering techniques like "interrogation in-depth" because they soon aroused accusations of "torture" which were investigated by a special commission headed by Sir Edmund Compton. The uproar over using "interrogation in-depth" on a small number of specially selected prisoners caught British military authorities off-guard since these techniques had been taught at the Joint Services Intelligence School for some time.[18]

Operational Lesson 6: Intelligence is even more critical in urban environments fighting paramilitary groups than in more conventional combat operations. Intelligence was critical since troops operating Belfast and Londonderry found themselves fighting an enemy in plain cloths which made them indistinguishable from the local population. Good information allowed the British military to selective target military operations against specific individuals. Good information also allowed the British to avoid humiliating mistakes like arresting old women, the physically infirmed, and pro-peace community leaders based on bogus tips anonymously supplied by the IRA disinformation operations. Unfortunately, the Royal Ulster Constabulary's intelligence-gathering capabilities in Catholic areas was virtually non-existent when the British Army intervened in 1969. Therefore the Army had to start building its own intelligence system from scratch which meant pouring in a large amount of money, men, and effort. Starting from scratch meant that it was along time before the British received the full return on their investment in intelligence-gathering activities. Eventually, however, they produced impressive results. The Director General of MI5 (British counterintelligence) estimates that security forces now prevent four out of every five attempted terrorist attacks in Northern Ireland.[19]

Tactical Lesson 6: Human intelligence was more important than technical intelligence in Northern Ireland and the responsibility for its collection rested at the battalion and company level. The paramilitaries offered fewer opportunities for technical collection than conventional military forces because of the nature of their organization and equipment. Consequently, the collection and evaluation of human intelligence became much more important. Increased need for human intelligence, and devolution of responsibility for its collection and assessment to battalion and company level, led to increasing the normal wartime compliment of the battalion intelligence section from 5 or 6 people up to 30 people.[20]

These lessons learned are valuable to any military planner. Each of the lessons provides greater insights into the military operations in Northern Ireland.

Planning Implications

From this case study, planners should consider the following implications for not considering extremist religious ideologies when developing strategies for military operations.

1. Failing to consider extremist religious ideology can lead to the development of a bad campaign design. Thorough analysis of every aspect of the operational environment is required in order to identify the right center of gravity and critical vulnerabilities. The extremist religious ideology may be the center of gravity or critical vulnerabilities. If planners fail to identify the right center of gravity or critical vulnerabilities, valuable time and resources will be wasted.

2. Engagement and wars are often prolonged because of the inability to properly target, insolate, or neutralize the extremist religious ideology or those who promulgate it. The conflict in Northern Ireland is a good example of this.

3. Mishandling of the extremist religious ideology can serve to fuel local support from "fence setters" and can excite terrorist activity. The planner must keep in mind that often time individuals or groups that support extremist religious ideologies are also prone to conduct robberies, bombings, assassinations, and other acts of terrorism to further their agenda. Factions in Northern Ireland such as the Real IRA have been linked to almost thirty attacks in Northern Ireland and other attacks in London.[21]

4. Execrating campaign or regional problems. The wrong or ineffective intelligence gathering methods could acerbate campaign problems. In the ongoing operation in Northern Ireland the British military found out that by abandoning some traditional approaches to suppressing riots, dealing with factions, and intelligence-

gathering prevented them from making humiliating mistakes like arresting or killing the wrong people. Mistakes like those can escalation tensions between the extremist, the local population, and those that are trying to legitimately combat the problem.

Extremist Religious Ideology in North Korea

This case study is important to the study because North Korea is currently an area that is internationally recognized as a potential place of future combat operations. On an annual basis, military exercises such as Ulchi-Focus Lens and Foul Eagle are conducted in the Republic of South Korea. Both Ulchi-Focus Lens and Foul Eagle are Republic of South Korea-US Combined Forces Command exercises. The exercises test the ability of the Republic of Korea to defend itself while being assisted by US armed forces. The insights presented in this case study can serve as a basis for additional study on the implications and impact of the extremist religious ideology of military operations in Northern Korea.

The Extremist Religious Ideology

The strength of North Korea is built in four areas: their relationship with China, the military, its president, and its religious ideology. For the purpose of this research, it is the president and the religious ideology that presents the extremist religious ideological dilemma.

The national government prescribes the populace to follow a religious practice called Juche. This belief is a mixture of Buddhism, Daoism, Shamanism, Confucianism, and Roman Catholicism, which teaches that every human being "bears divinity" and that one must "treat man as god."[22] Under this religious system, the local people respect the

president as god. An official description of the religious practice is listed below.

> Juche is the official state ideology of the Korean Workers Party ruling
> North Korea. The name is Korean and means *self-reliance*. It states that the
> subject of the revolution should be the masses, not any foreign power. It further
> develops that the nation must rely on itself; in this sense self-reliance. Juche is
> based on the teachings of Kim Il-sung.
> Juche has been promoted by the North Korean government and
> educational systemsince the term was first used in a 1955 speech by Kim Il Sung.
> At first, the ideology consisted of two fundamental ideas: that the proletarian
> revolution belonged to the people, and that man is the master of the revolution.[23]

On the surface, perhaps one may not see anything extreme about this religious

practice. One could even note the fact that the North Korean's constitution contains

provisions for freedom of religious belief. However, extremism exists because it is forced

on the populace and the North Korean government does not promote religious freedom as

outlined in the country's constitution.

Additionally, the practice of Juche is mentally and physically abusive. And it also

restricts the freedom of the North Korean people. According to the US State Department,

North Korea's government does not even actively pursue measures that prohibit the

beating, arrest, or killing of members of underground churches whose religious beliefs

are in opposition to those of Juche.[24] Michael Cromartie, Chairman, US Commission on

International Religious Freedom, reports that the North Korean government has

committed severe violations of human rights, including the extent to which the regime

attempts to control the very thoughts and beliefs of the North Korean people.[25]

Also, the US Department of State Bureau of Democracy, Human Rights and

Labor reported that some North Korean defectors claim that people from other religions,

namely Christians, were imprisoned and tortured for reading their Bibles and talking about God. They also reported that some people were subjected to biological warfare experiments.[26]

Finally, Juche is propagated by the government such that North Korean law reportedly mandates that picture of the "Great Leader," Kim IL Sung, and the "Dear Leader," Kim Jong IL, hang on the wall of every house, school room, and work place.[27] And the same report states that each village contains a Kim IL Sung Research Center where citizens are reportedly required to attend weekly meeting, watch inspirational films on the Dear Leader's life, and hold public confessions about political and moral failings.[28] The entire populace is acutely aware that the president and the government are in absolute control of all facets of politics and society. According to one report, the president's actions under the practice of Juche have created an environment of fear in which dissent of any kind is not tolerated and those that do so are subject to discrimination, arrest, imprisonment, torture, and sometimes execution by order of the government.[29]

In a concluding note, the Department of State has listed North Korea as one of seven countries that has state-sponsored terrorism.[30] The state sponsored and strictly enforced religious belief in North Korea is the extremist religious ideology called Juche. The next section outlines planning considerations and implications derived from this case study.

Planning Considerations

From this case study military planners should consider the following in relation to extremist religious ideologies when developing strategy for a military operation.

1. Power in the hands of a tyrant. The military planner should consider how the leader is using the extremist religious ideology to control the people. He should develop methods to isolate the leader before he encourages his follower and other sympathizers to rally behind his agenda.

2. There are implications associated with the suppression of personal freedom of thought and action. The military planner should be concerned about any extreme religious practice that prohibited personal freedom of thought. An extremist religious ideology that controls the mind of its subjects can cause or force the people to unite and focus towards a common goal or cause. As in the case of Kim Jong IL, the constant mind abuse could cause the people to have an abnormal belief in absolute allegiance to statehood and the president, such that the people commit their very lives to protect the interests of their nation as prescribed by the president.

3. The impact of state enforced religion. The planner must understand that a religion that is enforced by the state has intrinsic elements that have a tendency to be abusive both mentally and physically. State enforced uniformity of religious thought within a nation or civil state suppresses the individual will and gives too much power to a single individual or group. This can lead to corruption in other areas of society.

Planning Implications

From this case study, the most significant implication for not considering extremist religious ideologies is failure to properly target, isolate or marginalize the extremist leader or the extremist religious ideology in a timely manner can lead to a unification of effort between the leader and the populace. Such a leader could use that mind control as a method of coercing people to support the use of any weapon available including bomb strapped suicide attacks, kamikaze attacks, and even using nuclear weapons, all as a means of protecting and further the cause of a nation or ideological principle. With North Korea's strict adherence to Juche, the president could cause the people to commit one or all of the acts mentioned earlier in an effort to defeat any foe that threatens Republic of North Korea.

Extremist Religious Ideology in Kosovo

This case study is important because it describes how the US became possibly the first nation to proclaim international religious freedom as a part of its foreign policy. Also, the US military is used as the primary instrument of national power to enforce the foreign policy, military planners could find themselves developing operational plans that have extremist religious ideology as a Center of Gravity or a critical element to the operation.

Conflict in Kosovo

Kosovo is a country that has a history of ethnic problems. The most recent war between NATO and Serbia was the latest on a list of conflicts. This section analyzes the original battle of Kosovo that occurred in 1389 and how the religious implications of that war were prevalent in the NATO-led campaign against Kosovo.

In 1999, members of NATO launched a massive air bombing campaign against military targets in Serbia. The goal of the NATO operation was to enforce peace in the region and to provide humanitarian assistance. Military planners thought that the campaign would last only a couple of days and that the Serbian President, Slobodan Milosevic, would concede to the pressure of NATO. However, the campaign took a different course. According to one account, "the campaign was initially designed to destroy Serbian air defenses and high-value military targets . . . on the ground, the fighting worsened and within a week of the war starting, over 300,000 Kosovo Albanians had fled into neighboring Albania and Macedonia, with many thousands more displaced within Kosovo."[31] This outflow of refugees was alarming to the international community. It was even more troubling as reports suggested that many of the refugees were being threatened and even killed by the internal and external terrorist groups operating in Kosovo.

Some believe that the actions of the Kosovo Liberation Army (KLA) forces caused the government of Serbia to force the Albanians to make a mass exodus from Kosovo by using fear and terrorist tactics. The KLA was considered by the Albanians in Kosovo to be freedom fighters; the Serbs viewed them as terrorists. It has been documented that tens of thousands of Albanians were rounded up at gunpoint and loaded onto trains, before being dumped at the Macedonian border and other places.[32]

Initially, the KLA was only a couple of hundred insistent ethnic Albanians the Serbian government believed it could easily eradicate by using the Serbian Army. However, the government opted to use the Serbian police as a strategic move to undermine the importance of the KLA. During the forty-eight hours of fighting, more than forty civilians, including women and children, were killed in the fierce, indiscriminate fighting.[33] Unfortunately for the Serbians, their attempt to show the world that the KLA was defeated, served as an impetus for KLA recruitment. One report described the resulting actions as the following.

36

Thousands of young Albanians left their jobs, both in Kosovo and all across Western Europe where they had been working, to go and join the force fighting for the independence of their homeland: Kosovo. So rapid and unexpected was the inflow of recruits that the KLA initially was unable to cope. Many made their way into Drenica, which, despite the bitter defeats of February and March, was seen as the centre of the resistance. It is still not easy to understand how it was possible to bring together, organize and arm the 30,000 fighters that the KLA mustered between the spring and summer of 1998.[34]

The report goes on to say that the growth of the KLA was also caused by the close-knit family ties among clans. Albanians have always been regarded as impenetrable to outsiders and loyal to their own sense of unity.[35] The KLA was made up of radical youth, college students, teachers, doctors, members of influential families, army officers, and police inspectors.[36] Like many that are considered freedom fighters, the KLA fought for their freedom from the Yugoslavian government. Because their cause was for the freedom of the people, it is believed that many of the KLA fighters were from the adjacent countries of Albania, Yemen, and Saudi Arabia.[37]

Where is the religious extremism? The problem lies in a term called "Christolslavism."

The Extremist Religious Ideology

The idea of Christoslavism has been around since the original battle of Kosovo in 1389. The definition of Christolslavism is as follows:

> Christoslavism is the belief that Slavs are inherently Christian, and that any conversion of a Slav to another religion is a conversion of race or ethnicity: from Slav to Turk. Christoslavism involves a particular ideology of conversion that maintains that those Slavs who converted to Islam were the dregs of society, the cowards and the greedy, and by converting to Islam actually changed their ethnicity and race to Turkish.[38]

This ideology is supported by the belief that a famous Serbian prince was betrayed (like Christ) at the hands of the Turks. It is believed that the Turks pretended to

37

be Christians. The Christoslavism ideology suggest that Turks and Slavic Muslims should be treated as Christ-killers and bear an eternal and infinite guilt that takes away any claim they have to be considered human beings or to exist in Slavic areas.[39]

Christoslavism is also an ideology that supports "ethnic cleansing." It is believed that in the 1980's the civilian population in Bosnia experienced ethnic cleansing, genocide at the hands of Slobodan Milosevic, the president of Kosovo. It is further believed that this ideology was a part of the ideals of nation's leadership such that Milosevic supported terrorist groups such as the White Eagles, the Yellow Wasps, and Arkan's Tigers to conduct ethnic cleansings.[40] A description of each faction is listed below.

The White Eagles is an armed paramilitary Serbian group which participated in the Bosnian War. The group is believed to have been involved in war crimes committed in Bosnia-Herzegovina. It is also believed that they participated in ethnic cleansing, mass tortures, and killings.[41]

The Yellow Wasps is also a Serbian paramilitary group. They are believed to have conducted crimes such as murdering and torture of refugees and individuals with the civilian population.[42]

Arkan's Tigers was an element of the White Eagles paramilitary group. They called themselves the Serb Volunteer Guard "Tigers." It is believed that this group was responsible for the massacres over 1,400 people in Eastern Slavonia as part of a campaign of "ethnic cleansing" in the eastern area of Bosnia against Moslems.[43]

Perhaps the most solidifying act that showed that the Christoslavism ideology was supported by the government came when Slobodan Milosevic made a pilgrimage to a plan in Kosovo called the Polje. He made this trip in 1989 to mark the 600th anniversary

of the battle of Kosovo. The plain was the site of where the newly converted Muslim

Turks betrayed and killed the Christian Serbian prince. The leader proclaimed the

following statement before millions of Serbs.

> Six centuries ago, Serbia defended itself on Kosovo, but it also defended
> Europe. She found herself on the ramparts for the defense of European culture,
> religion and European society as a whole. They'll never do this to you again.
> Never again will anyone defeat you.[44]

Later, this became a central issue in the uprising in Yugoslavia (Croatia, Bosnia-

Herzegovina, and Macedonia) and the war in the Balkans. The war took a tremendous toll

on the Albanians that lived in Kosovo. After the atrocities that Milosevic brought upon

Albanians that lived in Kosovo, he was brought to justice for his crimes. His indictment

consisted of the following:

> Throughout Kosovo, the forces of the FRY and Serbia have harassed,
> humiliated, and degraded Kosovo Albanian civilians through physical and verbal
> abuse. Policemen, soldiers, and military officers have persistently subjected
> Kosovo Albanians to insults, racial slurs, degrading acts, beatings, and other
> forms of physical mistreatment based on their racial, religious, and political
> identification.[45]
> Beginning on or about 1 January 1999 and continuing until the date of this
> indictment, the forces of the FRY and Serbia, acting at the direction, with the
> encouragement, or with the support of Slobodan MILOSEVIC, Milan
> MILUTINOVIC, Nikola SAINOVIC, Dragoljub OJDANIC, and Vlajko
> STOJILJKOVIC, have utilized the means and methods set forth in paragraphs 92
> through 98 to execute a campaign of persecution against the Kosovo Albanian
> civilian population based on political, racial, or religious grounds.[46]

In summary, the religious problem was one that was deeply ingrained in the

minds and the nation's Christian leadership. They did not forget the incident that

happened almost 600 years ago. It appeared as if they purposefully set out to avenge the

loss of the Christian State, Kosovo, to the Turks who were Muslim. The next section

outlines planning considerations and implications derived from this case study.

Planning Considerations

From this case study, planners should consider the following in relation to extremist religious ideologies in strategy development.

1. The historical motives of the extremist religious group. The idea of Christoslavism has been around since the original battle of Kosovo in 1389. It is believed that Slobodan Milosevic harbored the old ideals in his mind as he made a pilgrimage to a place in Kosovo called the Polje. He made this trip in 1989 to mark the 600th anniversary of the battle of Kosovo. Planner should be students of history so that they can properly consider the historical issues associated with rival groups.

2. Extremists need external support, including moral and monetary. Support is often times a critical requirement. The planner should know that many extremist groups with religious ties often garner monetary and other support for each other. Some times support is received from transnational sources.

3. Many extremist religious ideologies are shrouded in myths. Myths are stories that are shared by a group, and which are a part of their cultural identity. As such, they are important to understand when looking at the history of a people.[47] Often myths are religious stories that involve the existence and activities of a supernatural being and they seek to explain at least some aspect of the origin or manner of things. Perhaps the most significant aspect of myths is the fact that they are believed to be true by those within the society.[48]

4. The importance of getting international support when attempting to execute a campaign against an extremist religious principle or a person or group that supports it. As in the Kosovo case, military planners knew the importance of getting support from an

40

international governing body such as the United Nations (UN) or NATO and building a coalition to combat Slobodan Milosevic, whose extremist actions were governed by his extremist religious ideological beliefs.

Planning Implications

Military planners should consider the following implications for not considering the implications of extremist religious ideologies in strategy development.

1. Failure to understand the historical nature associated with an extremist religious can lead to the creation of the wrong affect.

2. Failure to understand the nature of the ideology can lead to the death of hundreds even thousands of innocent civilians.

Extremist Religious Ideology in the Horn of Africa (Somalia)

This case study is important to the study of extremist religious ideology and military strategy because Somalia is rapidly regressing in a state of lawlessness because of economic decline and religious extremism. Additionally, the US military has already been sent to region to conduct military operations.

In 1991, US combat troops lead an international UN force to secure the environment for relief operations in Mogadishu, Somalia. Later, tensions in the region escalated such that several Pakistani soldiers were massacred which led to a US and UN troops attack on various targets in Mogadishu. The person behind the massacre and escalated tensions was a warlord named Mohamed Farrah Aidid.[49]

The forces that had been sent to the region to conduct peacekeeping operations were now at war against Aidid. One confrontation with Aidid cost the US the lives of eighteen soldiers and another eighty-four US soldiers were wounded.[50] Although this operation occurred over fourteen-year ago, the most interesting fact is that Somalia is still experiencing problems that require international aid and outside military intervention to help resolve its internal problems.

The operation in Somalia presents many lessons learned that are vitally important to current military planners. Somalia and the entire Horn of Africa remains flash point for future military operations.

The Extremist Religious Ideology

Shortly after the collapse of the Somali government in 1975, the country fell into a state of complete chaos. Different factions claimed power in different areas of the country. Warlords started to claim overall power and fighting and mayhem besieged the civil population. These warlords used their radical religious prowess to cause their followers to subdue all resistance by the struggling government and those that remained within the broken national security system.

The country had become a breeding ground because of the abounding poverty left in the wake of massive underemployment and a stifled national economy. People, especially young males, then viewed the radical factions the only organizations that could provide even their basic needs. The influence of the factions grew because they tended to be a voice for the people. These radical religious factions tended to capitalize on the support given to them by the impoverished Somali population.

For a long time, despite the internal oppression, the western countries did not immediately come to the aid of the oppressed people. This inaction allowed the warlords to continue their oppression of the civil population. One writer said, "The low profile, or state of near-absence of western powers in the affairs of Somalia has further encouraged radical religious leaders to seek the demise of any effort of reconciliation in the country."[51] This inaction allowed the radical leaders enough time to start instituting and enforcing their own form of government. This government included an imbalanced judicial system in which crime largely went unpunished and the proliferation of illegal weapons abounded. The failed state of Somali caused instability of the entire Horn of Africa region.

Somalia today is led primarily by a radical Islamic group called Al-Ittihad, a merger of Assalafiya and the Muslim Youth Union. This group provides education, social programs, employment opportunities, and other services to the populace. They also provide religious extremists established Islamic schools ranging from Koranic study centers to Islamic universities.[52] The education taught by this extremist group is arguably the leading contributor to the problems in Somalia. The leading teacher, Sheikh Ali Warsame, propagates Wahabbiya culture and philosophy to a majority Sunni population.

One report suggested that Al-Ittihad had been positioning itself since the late 1970's to take advantage of the deteriorating government. Al Ittihad campaigned for internal and external growth during the period between 1984 and 1991. The organization appealed to the disadvantaged and poor segments of the society. It is believe that they obtained positions in the civil service, the military, and academic institutions. There they proclaimed an Islamic awakening message that was in opposition to the government's agenda. Therefore, after the government collapsed, they emerged as a leader under the banner of Shar'ia Law. Although militant, they were successful in establishing Somalia as a true Islamic State.

43

Although Al-Ittihad controls the failed state, there are reports which suggest that the leadership is corrupt and is linked to several murders and kidnappings. One group of Al-Ittihad claimed responsibility for a series of bomb attacks in Addis Ababa in 1996 and 1997. The US government has accused Al-Ittihad of having ties with Al-Qaida.[53]

Obviously, it is clear to see that the country is a breeding ground for fundamentalist religious teachings of extremism and intolerance. The leadership of Somalia has ties to international terrorist groups and has allowed many to take refuge within its borders. The failed state has a proliferation of illegal drugs, guns, and crime. Although the Islamic fundamentalism and terrorism threatens the entire Horn of Africa region, the biggest problem is the devastation that it is causing on the civil population. The next section outlines planning considerations and implications derived from this case study.

Planning Considerations

From this case study, military planners should consider the following points relating to extremist religious ideologies when developing strategies for military operations.

1. Failed states are oftentimes the breeding ground for continued and new terrorist with extremist religious ideologies.

2. Factions and other groups with extremist religious ideologies will fight for power and territory.

3. Groups with extremist religious ideologies in failed states frequently have additional problems such as the proliferation of illegal drugs, guns, poverty, and crime.

4. Extremist religious groups need financing for long-term survival and growth.

5. When developing strategy to execute a campaign against a nation or other large group, plans must include the use of the other instruments of national power. This is important because the military alone is incapable of bring long term stability to a failed state.

Planning Implications

Planners should also consider the following implications for not accounting for extremist religious ideologies in strategy development.

1. Failure to understand the extent and intricacies of the extremist ideology can cause the planner to overlook the magnitude to the problem. The planner can fail to make critical connections such as the connection between the failing of a state and extremism. In this case study the Somalia became a safe haven that allowed extremists and their ideology to grow and thrive.

2. Failure to understand the extremist religious ideology can turn a good gesture into a local imbalance of power. In this case study, an act as simple as talking with and giving food to the wrong warlord was view by the locals as empowerment. This action caused an unintended balance of power in the area, which led to escalated tensions and eventually an armed conflict between UN forces and local warlords.

3. Failure to understand consider the extremist religious ideology can lead to the death of US, coalition, and allied forces. In 1992, eighteen US troops and a Nigerian soldier were killed during a fierce gun battle as tensions escalated in Mogadishu, Somalia.

In conclusion, the planner must consider everything possible about the enemy, including a possible extremist religious ideology. When the military planner fails to consider every possible dynamic about factions and groups whose actions are governed

by extremist religious ideologies, problems are repeatedly acerbated and the conflict can

be prolonged. Failure to properly consider the implications of extremist religious

ideologies can lead to the mission failure at every level: strategic, operational, and

tactical. Planners should carefully consider the essence of the saying by Sun Tzu, "If you

know the enemy and know yourself, you need not fear the result of a hundred battles. If

you know yourself but not the enemy, for every victory gained you will also suffer a

defeat."[54]

The next chapter examines some of the provisions that are current military

doctrine that specifically directs the planner to consider all aspect of extremist religious

ideology when developing military strategy.

---

[1]President of the United States, *A Record of Achievement, Ratification of the Fifteenth Amendment*, 30 March 1870 [document on-line]; available from http://www.grantstomb.org/civ/ exhciva.html; Internet; accessed on 12 May 2005.

[2]Leif E. Trondsen, "Ol' Satan's Church is Here Below," Southern Religion and Black Slavery in the Antebellum South [article on-line]; available from http://www.anglo catholic socialism.org/slavery.html; Internet; accessed on 3 January 2006.

[3]Ibid.

[4]Ibid.

[5]*The Holy Bible*, The First Scofield Study Bible, Ephesians 6:5-8, ed. C.I. Scofield (Belgium: World Bible Publishers, Inc., 1986).

[6]Trondsen.

[7]J. M. Shotwell, "Crystallizing Public Hatred, Ku Klux Klan Public Relations in the Early 1920's" (Thesis, University of Wisconsin, 1974), 219.

[8]Southern Poverty Law Center, A Hundred Years of Terror [report on-line]; available from http://www.iupui.edu/~aao/kkk.html; Internet; accessed on 16 January 2006.

[9]Ibid.

[10]Ibid.

[11]Ibid.

[12]Roger Kennedy, The Battle of the Boyne, A paper presented to the New York Military Affairs Symposium, CUNT Graduate Center, 11 June 2004; available from http://libraryautomation.com/nymas/boyne.html; Internet; accessed on 28 November 2005.

[13]Ibid.

[14]Landon Hancock, "Northern Ireland: Troubles Brewing," (Thesis, Institute for Conflict Analysis and Resolution, George Mason University, 1998) [thesis on-line]; available from http://cain.ulst.ac.uk/othelem/landon.htm; Internet; accessed on 2 December 2005.

[15]Council on Foreign Relations, Northern Ireland Loyalist Paramilitaries; available from http://cfrterrorism.org/groups/realira.html; Internet; accessed on 16 January 2006.

[16]Council on Foreign Relations, IRA Splinter Groups, 2005; available from http://cfrterrorism.org/groups/realira.html; Internet; accessed on 16 January 2006.

[17]Ibid.

[18]MOUT Lessons Learned Northern Ireland, Operational Lesson Learned 1; available from http://www.geocities.com/Pentagon/6453/nireland.html; Internet; accessed on 15 May 2006.

[19]MOUT Lessons Learned Northern Ireland, Operational Lesson Learned 6; available from http://www.geocities.com/Pentagon/6453/nireland.html; Internet; accessed on 15 May 2006.

[20]MOUT Lessons Learned Northern Ireland, Tactical Lesson Learned 6; available from http://www.geocities.com/Pentagon/6453/nireland.html; Internet; accessed on 15 May 2006.

[21]MOUT Lessons Learned Northern Ireland, Operational Lesson Learned 1; available from http://www.geocities.com/Pentagon/6453/nireland.html; Internet; accessed on 15 May 2006.

[22]Ibid.

[23]Wikipedia, Juche [encyclopedia on-line]; available from http://en.wikipedia.org/wiki/Juche; Internet; accessed on 27 September 2005.

47

[24]US State Department. 2002; [homepage]; available from http://www.state.gov/g/drl/rls/irf/2001/index.cfm?docid=553; Internet; accessed on 27 September 2005.

[25]Michael Cromartie, "United States Commission on International Religious Freedom" [article on-line]; available from http://www.uscirf.gov/events/cong_testimony/11152005_annualIRFrpt.html, accessed on 15 January 2006.

[26]Bureau of Democracy, *Human Rights and Labor, International Religious Freedom Report* [report on-line], U.S. Department of State; available from http://www.state.gov/g/drl/ rls/irf/2004/35335.htm; Internet; accessed on 16 January 2006.

[27]Ibid., 65.

[28]Ibid.

[29]US Commission on Internation Religious Freedom, *Annual Report of the United Stated Commission on International Religious Freedom*, May 2005 [report on-line]; available from http://www.uscirf.gov/countries/publications/currentreport/2005 annualRpt.pdf; Internet; accessed on 16 January 2006.

[30]Louis J. Freeh, Director, Federal Bureau of Investigation, Testimony before the United States Senate Committee on Appropriations, Armed Services, and Select Committee on Intelligence, 10 May 2001, "Threat of Terrorism to the United States;" available from http://www.fbi.gov/congress/congress01/freeh051001.htm; Internet; accessed on 23 May 2006.

[31]Michel Chossudovsky, *The KLA: A Mystery Wrapped in an Enigma*, 1999; available from http://www.antiwar.com/kla.html; Internet; accessed on 23 November 2005.

[32]Ibid.

[33]Ibid.

[34]Zoran Kusovac, "The KLA: Braced to Defend and Control," *Jane's Intelligence Review* (1999) [journal on-line]; available from http://www.janes.com/defence/news/kosovo/jir990401_01_n.shtml; Internet; accessed on 25 November 2005.

[35]Ibid.

[36]Ibid.

[37]Religious Tolerance.org, Religious Aspect of the Yugoslavia Kosovo Conflict Catholic peace group calls for prompt action to avert wider conflict in Kosovo, 20 May 1998; available from http://www.religioustolerance.org/war_koso.htm; Internet; accessed on 20 November 2005.

[38]Michael Sells, "Christoslavism 2/The Five Major Components," 1996; available from http://www.haverford.edu/relg/sells/postings/christoslavism2.html; Internet; accessed on 30 November 2005.

[39]Ibid.

[40]Ibid.

[41]John Pike, Federation of American Scientist, Intelligence Resource Services. *White Eagles Serbian Radical Party*, 3 October 1998; available from http://fas.org/irp/world/para/white_eagles.htm; Internet; accessed on 30 November 2005.

[42]Ilan Ziv, *Yellow Wasps: Anatomy of War Crimes*; available from http://www.frif.com/cat97/t-z/yellow_w.html; Internet; accessed on 30 November 2005.

[43]John Pike, Federation of American Scientist, Intelligence Resource Services, Serb Volunteer Guard [SDG / SSJ] "Arkan's Tigers;" 1 February 2000; available from http://www.fas.org/irp/world/para/sdg.htm; Internet; accessed on 30 November 2005.

[44]Slobodan Milosevic, Speech of Slobodan Milosevic at Kosovo Polje, translated by Tim Skorick, 24-25 April 1987; available from http://www.slobodan-milosevic.org/news/milosevic-1987-3-eng.htm; Internet; accessed on 18 November 2005.

[45]United Nations, The International Criminal Tribunal for the Former Yugoslavia, Case No. IT-99-37, The Prosecutor of the Tribunal against Slobodan Milosevic; available from http://www.un.org/icty/indictment/english/mil-ii990524e.htm; Internet; accessed on 28 November 2005.

[46]Ibid.

[47]Peter Kohler, *Urban Legends and Folklore*; available from http://ancienthistory.about.com/cs/grecoromanmyth1/a/whatismyth.htm; Internet; accessed on 15 May 2006.

[48]Ibid.

[49]Public Broadcast System, *Frontline*: "Ambush in Mogadishu" [article on-line]; available from http://www.pbs.org/wgbh/pages/frontline/shows/ambush/etc/cron.html; Internet; accessed on 18 May 2006.

[50]Ibid.

[51]A. Duale Sii arag, "The Birth and Rise of Al-Ittihad Al-Islami in the Somali Inhabited Regions in the Horn of Africa," 13 November 2005 [article on-line]; available from http://www.wardheernews.com/articles/; Internet; accessed on 2 December 2005

[52]Ibid.

[53]Ibid.

[54]Sun Tzu, *The Art of War*

CHAPTER 5

CURRENT US MILITARY DOCTRINE

> While the main laws of strategy can be stated clearly enough for
> the benefit of all and sundry, you must be guided by the actions of
> the enemy in attempting to secure a favorable position in actual
> warfare.[1]

Sun Tzu, *The Art of War*

The content of this chapter addresses the planner's responsibility to account for

extremist religious ideology when developing military from doctrinal prospective. It also

answers the secondary question: What is the current military doctrine relating to

extremist religious ideology? It also identifies doctrinal gaps.

This research includes the expert position of Michael Flynn, a military analyst

assigned to the Combined Arms Doctrine Directorate at Fort Leavenworth Kansas. It also

describes some of the provisions found in current military doctrine. The information

received from the military analysis is critical because the Combined Arms Doctrine

Directorate's mission is to develop, write, and update Army doctrine at the corps and

division level. The Combined Arms Doctrine Directorate provides doctrinal experts for

the Combat Training Centers, the Battle Command Training Program, and the Command

and General Staff College.[2]

The initial position is that since military forces are deploying on a routine basis to

support the Global War on Terrorism, there is adequate doctrine and provision therein

that directs the military planner to consider the extremist religious ideology of the people

in the current or projected area of operations. This being true, military planners should be doing a thorough job analyzing the extremist religious ideology of threat or enemy combatants within the identified area of operations.

Michael Flynn, military analyst with the Combined Arms Doctrine Directorate was asked the question: What are the doctrinal provisions that proscribes, directs or otherwise military planners to consider the implications of extremist religious ideologies when developing strategies for military operations? His reply is as follows:

> Command and Control doctrine in FM 3-0, 5-0, and 6-0 discusses the need for the commander to visualize and understand the environment to gain situational understanding. From a doctrinal standpoint, the Army uses the model of METT-TC (mission, enemy, terrain and weather, troops and support available, time available, civil considerations) as the major factors considered during mission analysis and throughout an operations. The Army also uses METT-TC as an information management tool . . . the major subject categories into which relevant information is grouped for military operations.
>
> On the Joint side, JP 3-0 and JP 5-0 (drafts) have develop what is know as a system perspective of the operational environment. The major systems in most operational environments are Political, Military Infrastructure, Information, Social and Economic.
>
> The staff (either joint or Army) assist the commander in understanding the environment. Estimates from the G/J-2 (Intel), IO, CMO, Chaplain, all consider information in the area of expertise to analyze that information and help the staff and commander understand the environment. Religion is part of that understanding. It falls under the C of METT-TC or Social in the Joint Construct.
>
> I anticipate that the next round of Army doctrine will address understanding religion as part of understanding the root of conflict in FM 3-13 (IO), FM 5-0 (Planning), and FM 6-0 (Command and control).[3]

From these statements by Mr. Flynn, it is deduced that current military doctrine generally includes provisions where the planner should account for extremist religious ideologies, however, most of which are implied, deduce or implicit. Arguably, planners should be intimately aware of the doctrinal provisions that are outlined in FM 3-0, FM 5-0, and FM 6-0. Planners should be aware of METT-TC and its utility in visualizing and describing the area of operations. Nevertheless, for the sake of analysis, each provision that Mr. Flynn identified are analyzed below.

The first doctrinal provision is found in JP 3-0. This JP discusses the Strategic

Estimate Process. Below is an excerpt from the publication:

> Combatant commanders develop and modify strategic estimates based on their assigned tasks after reviewing the strategic environment, the analysis of the various threats, the nature of anticipated operations, national and alliance strategic direction and forces available. Functionally oriented combatant commanders develop estimates for each theater they support.[4]

Perhaps the key phrase in this extract is, "reviewing the strategic environment, the

analysis of the various threats."[5] The implied task is for the military planner to conduct

analysis of the strategic environment and the threats therein. This includes collecting

information about the nature of the threats. Nature includes the extremist religious

ideologies as well as past, recent, and current actions by the enemy (factions and clans) in

the operational area. This descriptive view allows the planner flexibility in determining

what he believes is pertinent information requirement about the enemy. Since this

directive is general in nature, it only applies that extremist religious ideology is a part of

the strategic environment and that the planners should exhaust time and effort in

analyzing it.

The next doctrinal provision is in FM 3-0. This provision informs planners of the

requirement to visualize the battle space. Although visualizing the battle space is the

commander's responsibility, planners will assist him in the effort by providing estimates

and various other forms of analysis.

As mentioned by Flynn, the commander must conduct a myriad of actions after he

receives the mission. FM 3-0 directs the commander to consider the multiplicity of

implications in relation to the battlespace and then conduct a mission analysis that results

in their initial vision of the operation[6] Doctrine further states that commanders should use the factors of mission, enemy, terrain, troops, technology and civil (METT-TC), elements of operational design, staff estimates, input from other commanders, and their experience and judgment to develop their vision.[7] Although, the key word in this acronym is enemy, it is again descriptive in nature and not prescriptive. It does not specifically tell the commander or planner that extremist religious ideology should or must be an area of consideration. However, the FM does discuss mission analysis, staff estimates and things such as the Intelligence Preparation of the Battlefield (IPB) are a bit more prescriptive in nature.

METT-TC is important to planners because it serves as a guide that enables him (ultimately the commander) to consider all pertinent facets of the battle space. Of the six components, two are salient to the extremist religious ideology and strategy issue. Military doctrine prescribes that the planner, Intel planner, or others should consider the enemy and civil consideration when assessing the battle space.

The enemy component of METT-TC includes gathering and analyzing current information about his strength, location, activity, and capabilities. In stability operations this includes the analysis of adversaries, potentially hostile parties, and other threats to success.[8] Additionally, this analysis includes detail information of the enemy's strength, location, activity, and capabilities.

Civil considerations include gathering and analyzing information relate to civilian populations, culture, organizations, and leaders within the area of operation. The term culture is inclusive of religion, whether it is extremist or otherwise.

The next doctrinal provision is in FM 5-0. Among many things, this doctrinal provision discusses the IPB. This FM states that the intelligence system plans, directs,

54

collects, processes, produces, and disseminates intelligence on the threat and environment to perform IPB and the other intelligence tasks.[9] FM 2-0 provides the best definition of IPB. An extract from the definition is listed below.

> 1-11. IPB is the staff planning activity undertaken by the entire staff to define and understand the battlespace and the options it presents to friendly and threat forces. IPB includes input from the whole staff . . . It is a systematic process of analyzing and visualizing the threat and battlespace in a specific geographic area for a specific mission or in anticipation of a specific mission. To conduct effective IPB, the G2/S2 must--
> Identify characteristics of the AO, including the information environment, that will influence friendly and threat operations.
> Identify gaps in current intelligence holdings.
> Determine multiple enemy COAs (ECOAs) by employing predictive analysis techniques to anticipate future enemy actions, capabilities, or situations.
> Determine the enemy order of battle (OB), doctrine, and TTP. Identify any patterns in enemy behavior or activities.[10]

The IPB is perhaps the tool that is most prescriptive in nature. It not only directs the intelligence planner to know about the enemy and his impact on operations, it also seeks to identify information about the enemy that is required to fill intelligence gaps. Certainly, information about extremist religious ideology is a requirement for intelligence gathering and analysis. Yet, it seems to only be an implied are of study or analysis. There are no tasks in the IPB that clearly specifies extremist religious ideology should or must be an area of analysis.

FM 5-0 also states the following in relation to the standard military decision-making process. The following extract is taken from the regulation:

> 4 -27 Enemy. With the restated mission as the focus, Army leaders continue to analyze the enemy. For small unit operations, Army leaders need to know about the enemy's composition, disposition, strength, recent activities, ability to reinforce, and possible courses of action. They [leaders] determine what they do not know about the enemy, but should.[11]

This regulatory provision explicitly states that the commander should conduct an in-depth analysis of the enemy. This analysis should yield knowledge that will enable him to be in a position of advantage such that he can conduct predictive analysis of the enemy's possible courses of action. However, like the other provision, this one implies that the commander or planner will know that the impact of extremist religious ideological information is important enough to impact military operations. It seems that the onus is on the commander and planner to know what areas about the enemy are important and what the priority intelligence requirement questions to ask.

Additionally, FM 5-0 outlines the Chaplain as an additions source of input that assists the planner in receiving and analyzing information pertaining to extremist religious ideologies. The FM describes the Chaplain as a resource that supports the planning process by providing information about the effect of indigenous religions on military operations.[12]

The other document mention by Mr. Flynn is FM 6-0. Listed below is one of the key passages that support his earlier statement and position.

> 1-36. Commanders follow a continuous cycle of see first, understand first, act first, and finish decisively to decrease the options available to the enemy and create or preserve options for their own forces. Commanders, assisted by their C2 systems, aim to see first within the battlespace.[13]

While this passage gives the command and planner a frame work in which to conduct military operations, it does not definitively give planners any directive to include any aspect of extremist religious ideology in the planning equation. The understanding of the "see first" element of command and control certainly implies that the commander and planner should consider implications of the battlefield environment that will put him in a position of advantage while limited the options of the enemy.

Another FM that the Mr. Flynn did not mention is FM 1. Among many things, this FM describes the strategic environment and organization of the Army. It informs the planner of the general disposition of the enemy in the COE. The enemy is characterized as not only states but they are terrorists with extremist ideologies. It is implied that ideologies include extremist religious ideologies.

> 2-6. Today the Nation is fighting the War on Terrorism. In this war, adversaries are not only foreign states but also extremists employing irregular means. These adversaries seek to erode American power, influence, and resolve. They threaten the security of American society, endangering its freedoms and way of life. This war is fueled by an ideology that promotes intractable hatred of the democratic ideal, especially in its Western manifestations. It is likely to endure in some form for the foreseeable future . . . the National Security, National Defense, and National Military Strategies recognize traditional threats from other states and known adversaries. . . . In today's security environment, the Nation's overwhelming conventional and nuclear military superiority does not deter many emerging threats, especially followers of extremist ideologies who are willing to destroy themselves to achieve their aims.[14]

This extract seems to show that doctrine writers are acutely aware that extremists including those with extreme religious views are a part of the COE. They are aware that these extremist do not wage war in the traditional manner but in ways that may be uncommon to the Western way of waging war. Many are driven by extremist ideologies which cause them to conduct indiscriminate acts of terror and destruction as a way to bring about their desired end.

Out of all the military doctrine manuals mentions, this extract from FM 1 seems to come the closes to directing military planners to consider the implications of extremist religious ideologies when developing strategies for military operations. It seems to tell planners to collect information about all adversaries of the US that seek to disrupt American power, influence and resolve. It implies that planners at all levels should include extremist religious ideologies in their strategies.

In summary, military planners have doctrinal provisions that allow them to account for the threat dimension of warfare. Some of the provisions are included in JP 3-0, FM 1, FM 3-0, FM 5-0, and FM 6-0. These provisions include statements that direct military planners to collect information about enemy that will assist the commander in making visualizing the battle space and making decisions. These provisions are clear and accurate in outlining the nature and intent of extremist factions within the operational environment. These provisions are also explicit in directing planners to gather information relating to extremism, ethnic disputes, and religious rivalries.[15] However, it appears that theses provisions are general in nature and they seem to be associated with conventional warfighting. The doctrine associated with the military manuals listed earlier; seem to be associated with the kinetic fight and not necessarily with asymmetric warfare. Certainly the level and type of analysis required to conduct counterinsurgency operations would be different that fighting a tank battle in Iraqi desert.

In conclusion, although the doctrinal provisions identified; JP 3-0, FM 1, FM 3-0, FM 5-0, and FM 6-0, mention key words such as enemy, extremists, ideology, religion, and COE, they came up short in specifically addressing extremist religious ideology as a threat to military operations. It is further concluded that current military doctrine is not detailed or directive enough to be used by military planners to develop strategies to target, isolate, or naturalize extremist religious ideologies and those that propagate it. Mr. Flynn seemed to elude to this when he said, "I anticipate that the next round of Army doctrine will address understanding religion as part of understanding the root of conflict in FM 3-13 (IO), FM 5-0 (Planning), and FM 6-0 (Command and control)."[16] The next chapter addresses the primary research question: Do Army planners account for extremist

religious ideologies in the formulation of military strategy?

---

[1]Sun Tzu, *The Art of War*

[2]The Combined Arms Doctrine Directorate, Webpage; available from http://usacac.army.mil/CAC/CADD/index.asp; Internet; accessed on 20 May 2006.

[3]Michael Flynn, Military Analyst, C2 Division, Combined Arms Doctrine Directorate, Interview by author on 26 May 2006, Ft Leavenworth, KS.

[4]Joint Chief of Staff, Joint Publication 3-0, *Doctrine for Joint Operations* (Washington, DC: GPO, 1995), I-9.

[5]Ibid.

[6]FM 3-0, 5-10.

[7]Ibid.

[8]Ibid.

[9]US Army, Field Manual 5-0, *Army Planning and Orders Production* (Washington, DC: GPO, 2005).

[10]Headquarters Department of the Army, FM 2-0, *Intelligence* (Washington, DC: GPO, 2004), chapter 1-11

[11]US Army, Field Manual 5-0, 4-7.

[12]Ibid., c-4

[13]Headquarters, Department of the Army, Field Manual FM 6-0, *Mission Command: Command and Control of Army Forces* (Washington, DC: GPO, 2003), 30.

[14]Headquarters, Department of the Army, FM 1, *The Army* (Washington, DC: GPO, 2005), 6 and 2-10.

[15]Headquarters, Department of the Army, Field Manual 5-0, par 1-26.

[16]Flynn.

CHAPTER 6

ANALYSIS OF SURVEY

With many calculations, one can win; with few one cannot. How much less chance of victory has one who makes none at all![1]

Sun Tzu, *The Art of War*

This chapter examines the outcome of first hand research conducted to answer the question: Do Army planners at the operational and tactical levels account for extremist religious ideologies in the formulation of military strategy?

Those that were interviewed included randomly selected officers attending SAMS at Fort Leavenworth, Kansas and officers who recently returned from service in various theaters of operations including Iraq, Afghanistan, and Kosovo.

The position of the officers who are attending SAMS is critical because these officers will play a critical role in future operational and tactical level planning. The officers who graduate from the year-long Advanced Military Studies Program are trained and educated in military art and science at the graduate level and are developed to be future commanders and General Staff officers with the abilities to solve complex problems in peace and war. These officers will eventually become the focal point for the development of strategy and plans for operational and tactical level operations and missions.

The position of the officers who recently returned from deployment is important because their experience provides insights into how operations are currently being performed. These officers have first hand experience in the formulation and execution of operation orders either generated at their headquarters or sent to them from their higher

headquarters. These officers were recently deployed to either Iraq or Afghanistan.

Each officer listed in the survey was asked to provide answers to the same seven

questions. An analysis of the answers to the survey questions is outlined below.

Question 1: Should military planners at the operational and tactical levels

consider the extremist religious ideology of the enemy when developing strategy for

military plans?

Survey Answer: Yes

Analysis: All eight of the officers surveyed overwhelmingly agreed that military

planners at the operational and tactical levels should consider the extremist religious

ideology of the enemy when developing strategy for military plans. One person stated

that planners at the operational and tactical levels should understand the dynamic

challenges presented by extremist organizations. He said that these challenges should be

codified into guidance so that the tactical level commander can properly execute his

missions.

Question 2: Should information about extremist religious ideology be included in

operation orders?

Survey Answer: Yes

Analysis: Again, all eight of the officers surveyed agreed that information about

extremist religious ideology should be included in operation orders. One officer stated

that the information concerning extremist organizations should be included in division

and below Operation Orders. He said that the information may be captured in the form of

CCIR [Commanders Critical Information Requirement], targeting guidance and as part of the ISR [Intelligence Surveillance and Reconnaissance] plan. He also said that another possibility of capturing (information) about these organizations is to link them sequentially through time, space, and mission requirements. He further said that at the Corps and above level, information about extremist organizations is articulated in various products concerning the area of operations (JAOI [Joint Area of Operations]).

Question 3: What is the utility, if any, of knowing information about the enemy's extremist religious ideology?

Analysis: The SAMS Planners seem to indicate that the utility of knowing information about the enemy's extremist religious ideology enables planners to better understand the enemy. They suggest that knowing the enemy is a part of knowing the terrain and the environment. It is further suggested that this information is an intricate part of knowing the culture of the enemy and by knowing the enemy's culture the planner can better target the his critical capabilities, critical requirements and critical vulnerabilities.

Survey Answers:

SAMS 1: "Religious ideology is vital to a holistic understanding of the enemy from an IPB perspective particularly in the COE [Contemporary Operational Environment] we operate in today. Ideology is a key fundamental [aspect] to mass mobilization as it is a viable cause."[2]

SAMS 2: "The adversary "extremist" is part of the environment; a detailed understanding of his CC [Critical Capability], CR [Critical Requirement], and CV [Critical Vulnerability] will allow operational/tactical level planners to understand their battlefield geometry. This geometry is based on their mission, time analysis, space "area of operation" and forces available."[3]

SAMS 3: "Religious ideology/slant just like ethnic/cultural information provides assistant with Cultural IPB [Intelligence Preparation of the Battlefield]."[4]

SAMS 4: "We preach know the terrain/ environment, know the enemy, know yourself." Religious ideology is part of knowing the terrain/ environment. Religious ideology is what drives terrorist organizations as well as Islamic practitioners that are potential allies of US operations. The more we understand the enemy (and potential ally) values and thought processes, the more effectively we can plan IO [Information Operations] and kinetic operations."[5]

Iraq 1: "The more information that any solider, Marine, or U.S. service man or woman can know about the Islamic extremist the better. We must learn more about the religion of Islam and the various fundamentalist sects within Islam. This knowledge should be disseminated throughout the chain of command; for example, from the brigade to the squad and fire team level. The utility of knowing this information lies in truly understanding the enemy in a pure Sun Tzu manner, but more importantly it bifurcates Islam and Islamic fundamentalism."[6]

Iraq 2: "It fits most appropriately into situational awareness and as a consideration for planners that are determining desired effects and supporting tasks--part of the battlefield environment. The highest utility is always the ability to accurately predict outcomes based on a factor's influence."[7]

Afghanistan 1: "Yes, it should be considered as it will help you to better anticipate the enemy's response under certain circumstances."[8]

Afghanistan 2: "As an MI [Military Intelligence] officer, I believe it one of the many significant factors that must be taken into consideration when attempting to gain a true picture of the enemy --his short and long-term goals, how he is likely to react to given situations--how we can exploit this."[9]

Question 4: Have you ever received information about the extremist religious ideology of an enemy or opposing force from a military planner for any operation you have participated in? Was the information adequate enough?

Analysis: Conditions within the current operational environment has caused military planners to be more aware of the nature of extremist ideologies. The results of the survey suggest that officers (and all Soldiers) who deploys in support of Operation Enduring Freedom and Operation Iraqi Freedom receive information about the extremist religious ideology of the people and the enemy within those theaters of operation.

Additionally, the results of the survey suggest that old contingency plans may not directly include information about extremist religious ideologies. Exercise data for some regions that are non-hostile, also may not explicitly outline information about extremist religious ideologies.

Survey Answers:

SAMS 1: "Yes, during exercises in SAMs however it was very shallow."[10]

SAMS 2: "Any information I received during exercises that dealt with extremist ideology was critically analyzed against what our mission."[11]

SAMS 3: "Yes. Have all been exercises at CGSC/SAMS. I felt the information related to religious ideology was adequate for continuing planning/consideration."[12]

SAMS 4: "No. It was not a part of contingency planning for Eighth Army. Even CGSC/ SAMS exercises, such information was only part of the "background book." To my recollection, such information was not part of the OPORD [Operation Order]/CJCS WARNORD [Chairman, Joint Chief of Staff Warning Order]/COCOM WARORD [Combatant Commander Warning Order]/OPLAN [Operations Plan]/etc."[13]

Iraq 1: "We received information about the local religious hierarchy when we conducted Operation Badlands. This was the operation that took A Company from 1st BN [Battalion], 6th Marines into the small village of Saqlawiyah. Saqlawiyah was suburb to the city of Fallujah. The information was not complete, and due to a lack of intelligence we truly did not have a clear picture of the local imams and sheiks in the village. The prevailing thought was that we would establish a forward operating base in Saqlawiyah in order to collect this information and similar information about the village. Without a clear intelligence picture and paired with an inherent bias that all imams and sheiks are sympathetic to the "muj" or insurgent cause, all persons of religion were treated guilty until proven innocent. Quite frankly, the military in general simply does not understand the religion of Islam or any religion outside of Christianity for that matter; therefore we can not and do not plan accordingly."[14]

Iraq 2: N/A

Afghanistan 1: "Yes, in Afghanistan we were warned about extremists and we factored into our decision making process. In this case, how to respond if faced with possible capture by AQ [al Queda] or Taliban forces. Don't know if it was adequate since none of us had to face such a situation, but it was taken into consideration."[15]

Afghanistan 2: "Yes--as part of our train up for, during, and our de-briefings following OEF 5. The initial information prior to going into the box was fairly non-specific and geared toward any audience. Given my branch and responsibilities, I felt it necessary to research the topic more and provide add'l info to my staff."[16]

Question 5: When developing a strategy for an operation, what considerations, if any, should you as an operational and tactical level planner give to the possibility of the enemy having an extremist religious ideology?

Analysis: The officers supplied a thorough list of things planners should consider when there is knowledge of the enemy having an extremist religious ideology. The SAMS planners listed the following:

1. The implications associated with combat in urban areas

2. The planner must attempt to discover if the extremist religious ideology is the enemy's Center of Gravity.

3. Understanding that to combat this action supports the framework of the National Security Strategy and the National Military Strategy

4. Understanding possible lines of operations associated with the extremist religious ideology

5. The employment of an information operation campaign to shape operations against the extremist ideology

6. What allies are available from the religious community (Muslim)?

The considerations listed by the officers with recent experience from the current theaters of operation list were similar to the list from the SAMS officers. The answers from these officers are more exclusive and seem to directly apply to current operations.

1. Planners should pay particular attention to militant religious extremist.

2. Planners must get accurate information through HUMINT [Human Intelligence] collection sources.

3. Extremist attracts new recruits or followers.

4. Planners should always look for ways of exploitation. Look to find how the ideology is spreading.

5. Who are the main sources of the extremist ideology?

6. Know what resources and options that is available to counter the extremist beliefs

7. Looks for reasons why the ideology is spreading.

8. What is the root causes of the extremist ideology?

So what does this mean? These lists show that many officers are quite knowledgeable of the fact that extremist religious ideologies presents various implications that impact the strategy associated with military operations. They are also aware of many of the issues that planners must take into consideration when developing operational and tactical plans.

Survey Answers:

SAMS 1: "From my perspective, in many cases religious ideology is a center of gravity (COG). I have seen a transition from winning hearts and minds as a focus, however, I think if you dig a look a layer deeper into what motivates the people to support extremist organizations you will find a common theme of religion."[17]

SAMS 2: "All operations being conducted have at its core the [*National Security Strategy*] 2004, and NMS [*National Military Strategy*] 2002 fundamental of defeating extremist religious organizations and to promote peace."[18]

SAMS 3: "Exercise (but I would use the same thought process for Real World)-- ideology (extremist, ethnic, national, religious--whatever) consists of attitudes and beliefs of either an individual or group. If your operations occur within an area populated by people with a significantly different/opposed belief system than yours, you must take that into account, especially if you will be operating in that area for an extended period of time. Ideally, you should seek to co-opt (best case) members of the population to support your operations or remain neutral (draw). However, shaping opinions/behaviors requires a great deal of effort and time. [See Robert Gagne's, The Conditions of Learning and the Theory of Instruction, 4th ed. (Fort Worth: Holt, Rinehart, and Winston, Inc, 1985), 219-230 and 232 and Kim Cragin and Scott Gerwehr, Dissuading Terror: Strategic Influence and the Struggle Against Terrorism, (Santa Monica, California: Rand Corporation, 2005), 19-20 for info on the challenges of influence/attitude shaping.]"[19]

SAMS 4: "Exercise and Real World: As stated in question #3, understanding extremist religious ideology is part of understanding the environment and understanding the enemy. As a planner, I would use my understanding of extremist ideology to conduct center of gravity analysis, inform development of lines of operation, develop my IO [Information Operations] campaign, and search for potential allies from the Muslim community."[20]

Iraq 1: "All the consideration in the world should be built into the planning simply because the extremist religious ideology is the militant arm of religious group; thus the

68

enemy that we are fighting. Therefore, to not consider the extremist religious ideology would be foolish. However, in order to build this information into the operation, the planners must have accurate information in order to plan accordingly. That information can only be obtained through sound HUMINT [Human Intelligence] collection and the exploitation (HET) of various groups that are interacting with the local population on a daily basis; for example, Civil Affairs teams, local Iraqi contractors, Iraqi elected officials such as city council members, mayors, etc."[21]

Iraq 2: "Again, the key is to determine the impact--it is not important if it does not impact the operation. Extremist religious ideology does impact operations, but not necessarily in a direct manner. It is important to distinguish between religion as a root cause and as a category to be used by the enemy for IO [Information Operations]."[22]

Afghanistan 1: "Extremists (TRUE EXTREMISTS) in my opinion--based on antidotal information--seem to surrender less often than soldiers. This makes for what a Westerner would consider an irrational enemy."[23]

Afghanistan 2: "Basic tenets of the extremist religion; what, if any, appeal does it have for recruits, the population; how does it differ from mainstream religions of the region; can these seams be exploited; how is the ideology spread; who are the primary authors of the ideology; what measures are available to friendly forces that legitimately counter these beliefs; why has the ideology spread; what are the root causes that drive the disaffected to believe and can these be addressed; etc."[24]

Question 6: What military doctrinal provision directs (or suggests) military planners to gather, analyze, and disseminate information about extremist religious ideologies when developing strategies for an operation?

69

Analysis: Most of the officers who completed the questionnaire did not readily know any doctrinal provisions that direct military planners regarding extremist religious ideologies. However, one of the SAMS officers listed several sources which included JP 2-01.3, *Joint Tactics, Techniques, and Procedures for Joint Intelligence Preparation of the Battlespace,* II-38. This reference clearly states that the intelligence analysis should consider both civilian and military populations including significant factors such as population patterns, living conditions, ethnic conflicts and rivalries, languages and dialects, cultural and class distinctions, political attitudes, religious beliefs, educational levels, and any existing or potential refugee situations. It is concluded that basic information regarding how planners should account for and regard extremist religious ideology is imbedded in the SAMS curriculum.

Survey Answers:

SAMS 1: "I don't know of any that specifically address the aspects of religion mentioned. But I have seen emerging doctrine that includes culture and a subset of culture is religion."[25]

SAMS 2: "I am unaware of such doctrine, not to say that it does not exist. I would look toward the JTF SoSA people; they develop PMESIIs for various parts of the world and provide MOE for the initial development of tasks."[26]

SAMS 3: "JP 2-0, *Doctrine for Intelligence Support to Joint Operations*, 9 March 2000--JIPB definition:

- JP 2-01.3, *Joint Tactics, Techniques, and Procedures for Joint Intelligence Preparation of the Battlespace*, II-38 discusses "religious and cultural impact" under the discussion about the Human Dimension

- Appendix K, JP 3-05.1, *Joint Tactics, Techniques, and Procedures for Joint Special Operations Task Force Operations* discusses Intelligence requirements including religious/cultural information

- Joint Publication 3-57, *Joint Doctrine for Civil-Military Operations* addresses the need to assess the post conflict environment (I-19).

- JP 3-07.3, *Peace Operations* (Revised Final Draft) (I-42)."[27]

<u>SAMS 4</u>: "Off the top of my head, I don't believe any doctrinal manual directs military planners to analyze religious ideologies."[28]

<u>Iraq 1</u>: Unknown.

<u>Iraq 2</u>: "I don't know, but I believe the Intel shop covers this under the estimate and IPB. The last check is done in wargaming in MDMP [Military Decision Making Process] when the two shop provides "red team" analysis."[29]

<u>Afghanistan 1</u>: "I think this is covered under basic IPB [Intelligence Preparation of the Battlefield] doctrine (FM 34-130)."[30]

<u>Afghanistan 2</u>: "Cultural IPB found in both Joint & Army Urban Operations manuals."[31]

<u>Question 7</u>: Knowing what you know now about extremist religious ideology, if you had to develop a strategy for an operational or tactical level operation, how would you account for the possibility of an extremist religious ideology?

<u>Analysis</u>: The SAMS officers suggest that information about the extremist religious ideology is very important. Planners should solicit the assistance of anthropologist, historians and even religious leaders. The three planners with recent deployment experience reintegrated the need to work through the Civil Affairs Teams to build relationships with local religious leaders and seek to gather their assistance in gaining intelligence about religious extremists. Those planners also suggested that there

71

is a need to account for everything on the battlefield, including extremist beliefs and how best to target them.

Survey Answers:

SAMS 1: "Again, religion is critical to seeing the enemy and the IPB [Intelligence Preparation of the Battlefield] process. In my mind, understanding culture (religion) is critical."[32]

SAMS 2: "In developing a strategy to counter extremist ideologies, I would coordinate with an existing SoSA , anthropologist, historian and religious leader from within that initial community to gain a deeper understanding of what the problem is. Importantly to see how the individual is able to operate within the physical and spiritual dimensions based on his beliefs. A new strategy may not be the answer to defeat an intangible variable."[33]

SAMS 3: "When the J-2 [Joint Intelligence] conducts JIPB [Joint Intelligence Preparation of the Battlefield], one of the aspects includes cultural IPB [Intelligence Preparation of the Battlefield]. Must take into account the effects our operations may or may not have on local popular perceptions/support. Extremist religious ideology is not always "bad"--some liberals in the U.S. would argue that conservative, Christian organizations exhibit 'extremist/religious ideology'--must seek to avoid stereotyping and base operations on the local situation/environment."[34]

SAMS 4: See my response to question #5. [35]

Iraq 1: "See question 5. Of course, you would need to draw heavily upon your intelligence collection. In addition, I would rely heavily upon the civil affairs group or team. They hold the resident religious experts or have gathered information about the objective area due to relationships they have established. Shifting the paradigm

concerning the way we fight and plan today, why could we not have civilian religious

experts (possibly contractors) that are involved the operational planning in order to fill

the gap of our intellectual shortfalls? Religious sensitivities are so important, especially

in the Islamic world. We must consider these sensitivities and work them into every

operation that is planned."[36]

Iraq 2: "Again IPB [Intelligence Preparation of the Battlefield]. The key here is

maximum use of TENCAP [Tactical Exploitation of National Capabilities]. Too often

decisions are made in a partial vacuum without taking advantage of research and

knowledge that already exists at the national level. This highlights the importance of true

"all source" analysis and maximizing the leverage achieved through work done by

experts and integrating current ground level information from tactical sources (guys on

the ground)."[37]

Afghanistan 1: "Extremists often must be killed or captured versus negotiating

with them. The very definition of an extremist (somebody who holds extreme or radical

political or religious beliefs) means someone who cannot be reasoned with. The whole

Geneva Convention system is founded on reason and the avoidance of needless suffering.

Extremists offer planners a real challenge in this regard."[38]

Afghanistan 2: "When I assess enemy capabilities, intent, and probable courses of

action, I have to account for any and everything that affects the CJOA [Combined Joint

Operations Area], including extremist beliefs and how best to target them."[39]

---

[1]Sun Tzu, *The Art of War*

[2]Joseph Pepper, Interview by author on 23 April 2006, Ft Leavenworth, KS.

[3]Joseph Bookard, Interview by author on 23 April 2006, Ft Leavenworth, KS.

[4]Eric Anderson, Interview by author on 23 April 2006, Ft Leavenworth, KS.

[5]David London, Interview by author on 23 April 2006, Ft Leavenworth, KS.

[6]Christopher Phelps, Interview by author on 23 April 2006, Ft Leavenworth, KS.

[7]Michael Giglione, Interview by author on 14 May 2006, Ft Leavenworth, KS.

[8]David King, Interview by author on 23 April 2006, Ft Leavenworth, KS.

[9]Deitra Korando, Interview by author on 23 April 2006, Ft Leavenworth, KS.

[10]Joseph Pepper, Interview by author on 23 April 2006, Ft Leavenworth, KS.

[11]Joseph Bookard, Interview by author on 23 April 2006, Ft Leavenworth, KS.

[12]Eric Anderson, Interview by author on 23 April 2006, Ft Leavenworth, KS.

[13]David London, Interview by author on 23 April 2006, Ft Leavenworth, KS.

[14]Christopher Phelps, Interview by author on 23 April 2006, Ft Leavenworth, KS.

[15]David King, Interview by author on 23 April 2006, Ft Leavenworth, KS.

[16]Deitra Korando, Interview by author on 23 April 2006, Ft Leavenworth, KS.

[17]Joseph Pepper, Interview by author on 23 April 2006, Ft Leavenworth, KS.

[18]Joseph Bookard, Interview by author on 23 April 2006, Ft Leavenworth, KS.

[19]Eric Anderson, Interview by author on 23 April 2006, Ft Leavenworth, KS.

[20]David London, Interview by author on 23 April 2006, Ft Leavenworth, KS.

[21]Christopher Phelps, Interview by author on 23 April 2006, Ft Leavenworth, KS.

[22] Michael Giglione, Interview by author on 14 May 2006, Ft Leavenworth, KS.

[23]David King, Interview by author on 23 April 2006, Ft Leavenworth, KS.

[24]Deitra Korando, Interview by author on 23 April 2006, Ft Leavenworth, KS.

[25]Joseph Pepper, Interview by author on 23 April 2006, Ft Leavenworth, KS.

[26]Joseph Bookard, Personal Survey. 23 April 2006, Ft Leavenworth, KS..

[27]Joseph Anderson, Interview by author on 23 April 2006, Ft Leavenworth, KS.

[28]David London, Interview by author on 23 April 2006, Ft Leavenworth, KS.

[29]Michael Giglione, Interview by author on 14 May 2006, Ft Leavenworth, KS.

[30]David King, Interview by author on 23 April 2006, Ft Leavenworth, KS.

[31]Deitra Korando, Interview by author on 23 April 2006, Ft Leavenworth, KS.

[32]Joseph Pepper, Interview by author on 23 April 2006, Ft Leavenworth, KS.

[33]Joseph Bookard, Interview by author on 23 April 2006, Ft Leavenworth, KS.

[34]Joseph Anderson, Interview by author on 23 April 2006, Ft Leavenworth, KS.

[35]David London, Interview by author on 23 April 2006, Ft Leavenworth, KS.

[36]Christopher Phelps, Interview by author on 23 April 2006, Ft Leavenworth, KS.

[37]Michael Giglione, Interview by author on 14 May 2006, Ft Leavenworth, KS.

[38]David King, Interview by author on 23 April 2006, Ft Leavenworth, KS.

[39]Deitra Korando, Interview by author on 23 April 2006, Ft Leavenworth, KS.

CHAPTER 7

CONCLUSION

> The strategy of the enemy in short, is to terrorize, intimidate, and tear down. A strategy with short term advantage because it is easier to tear down than to build up.[1]

The primary question that this research sought to answer was: Do Army planners at the operational and tactical levels account for extremist religious ideologies in the formulation of military strategy? The perceived problem and initial position was military planners are not doing a thorough job analyzing the extremist religious ideology of threat or enemy combatants within the contemporary operating environment, yet they are developing strategies and issuing orders that should entail information about their ideology. The secondary questions were:

1. What must planners consider in relation to extremist religious ideologies?

2. What are the implications of not accounting for religious ideologies in strategy development?

3. What is the current military doctrine relating to the subject?

The content of chapter 4 established the foundation for the research and it provided answers for some of the secondary questions. This chapter presented case studies involving factions and groups with extremist ideologies during the post reconstruction period in the US; and others in Northern Ireland, in Kosovo, and in Somalia (Horn of Africa). The actions by those groups clearly solidified the need for current military planners to consider the multiplicity of extremist religious ideological issues when developing the strategy for plans and operations.

The contents of this chapter also provided answers to the secondary question: What must planners consider in relation to extremist religious ideologies and what are the implications of not accounting for religious ideologies in strategy development? Succinctly speaking, the military planner must consider everything about the enemy including his religion and those that espouse or propagate an extremist religious ideology. Failure to properly consider the implications can lead to the failure the mission at every level: strategic, operational, and tactical.

Chapter 5 presented answers to the secondary question: What is the current military doctrine relating to the subject? The answer to this question is summarized to include JP 3-0, FM 1, FM 3-0, FM 5-0, and FM 6-0. Although, doctrine found in these manuals describes the COE and directs the planner to gather information about the enemy that could affect plans and strategies such as information such as extremism, ethnic disputes and religious rivalries. They do not specifically state the term extremist religious ideologies nor do they direct the military planner to specifically account for them when developing military plans. The provisions found in these manuals relating to extremist religious ideology are descriptive and not prescriptive.

Chapter 6 directly addresses to the primary research question: Do Army planners at the operational and tactical levels account for extremist religious ideologies in the formulation of military strategy? This question was answered using information received from survey questions presented to officers who are attending SAMS and officers with recent deployment experience in Afghanistan and Iraq. The results of the interviews suggest that military planners at the operational and tactical levels are considering extremist ideological information about the enemy when they develop strategy of operations and missions.

The officers that are attending SAMS, future operational and tactical level planners, are being taught to consider everything possible about the enemy, the terrain, and the operational environment when developing plans for military operations. The officers with current combat experience reported that it is almost common practice for military planners to consider and include aspects about the enemy's religious ideology. Specifically, Military Intelligence planners are considering the implications of extremist religious ideologies as they conduct Intelligence Preparation of the Battlefield.

Now, after considering all the information gathered within this research, the final conclusion is military planners at the operational and tactical level are accounting for extremist religious ideologies in the formulation of military strategy. They are doing this within the framework already established in operational procedures within exercise procedures and those that prescribed by commanders within the various AORs. However, the contention rests in the adequacy of the planning conducted by the military planners. The planning is not adequate. Planners are not conducting analysis that is thorough enough to successfully target, isolate, or neutralize extremist religious ideologies and those that propagate them.

This problem is not one that suggests planners are incompetent; rather the problem has its origin in the adequacy of military doctrine. Current doctrine such as JP 3-0, FM 1, FM 3-0, FM 5-0, and FM 6-0 mentions key words such as enemy, extremists, ideology, religion, and COE but fails to specifically address extremist religious ideology as a threat to military operations. The doctrine therein fails to proscribe specific measures to insure that planners consider the implication of extremist religious ideologies on military operations. Although, the IPB and MDMP includes enemy considerations, there are no specific tools identified in these manuals that specifically causes the planner to factor in the impact of extremist religious ideology such that successful strategies can be developed to target, isolate, or neutralize them and those that propagate them. New doctrine that specifically addresses the issue of extremist religious ideology must be introduced. This doctrine will serve to guide and direct military planners at the operational and tactical levels in analyzing the extremist religious ideology of threat or enemy combatants within the contemporary operating environment. It will also help planners develop better strategies for military operations.

---

[1]National Security Strategy for Victory in Iraqi

BIBLIOGRAPHY

Books

Braun, Aurel, and Scheinberg Stephen. *The Extreme Right: Freedom and Security at Risk*. Oxford, West View Press, 1997.

Esposito, John L. *The Islamic Threat: Myth or Reality*. New York, Oxford University Press, 1999.

Cobb, Ronald Lee. *Memories of Bosnia*. Bloomington, IN: AuthorHouse Publishers, 2004.

Gvosdev, Nikolas K., and Ray Takeyh. *The Receding Shadow of the Prophet: The Rise and Fall of Radical Political Islam*. Westport, CT: Greenwood Publishing Group, Inc., 2004.

Hill, Sean D. *Extremist Groups: An International Compilation of Terrorist Organizations, Violent Political Groups, and Issue-Oriented Militant Movements*. Huntsville TX: Office of International Criminal Justice and the Instituted for the Study of Violent Groups, Sam Houston State University, 2002.

Hunt Michael H. *Ideology and U. S. Foreign Policy*. New Haven: Yale University Press, 1987.

Lumbard, Joseph E. B. *Islam, Fundamentalism, and the Betrayal of Tradition*. Canada: World Wisdom, Inc., 2004.

Marshall, Charles B., and William V.Obrien. *Counterinsurgency: Some Problems and Implications*. New York: The Council on Religion and International Affairs, 1969.

McManus Dole, and Robin Wright. *Flashpoint: Promise and Peril in a New World*. New York: Random House Inc, 1991.

Outman, James L., and Lisa M. Outman. *Terrorism Almanac*. New York: Thomson Gale Publishers, 2003.

Periodicals

"Are Islamist Schools a Threat to U.S.?" *USA Today* 133, no. 2715 (December 2004): 6.

"International: The Suffocating Limits of Reform; Saudi Arabia London." *The Economist* 375, no. 8427 (21 May 2005): 65.

Hughes, John. "Turbulent Indonesia, Moderate Islam." *Christian Science Monitor* (14 April 2004): 9.

Shotwell, J. M. "Crystallizing Public Hatred, Ku Klux Klan Public Relations in the Early 1920's." Thesis, University of Wisconsin, 1974.

Zaidi, Hasan. "Over To The General; Monitoring Madarsas-Potential Breeding Grounds for Extremism-is As Serious a Challenge for Musharraf as Reining in Militants." *India Today* (1 August 2005): 58.

Government Documents

Headquarters, Department of the Army. Field Manual 1, *The Army*. Washington, DC: GPO, 2005.

_____. Field Manual 3-0, *Operations*. Washington, DC: GPO, 2001.

_____. Field Manual 5-0, *Army Planning and Orders Production*. Washington, DC: GPO, 2005.

_____. Field Manual FM 6-0, *Mission Command: Command and Control of Army Forces*. Washington, DC: GPO, 2003.

Joint Chiefs of Staff. Joint Publication 3-0, *Doctrine for Joint Operations*. Washington, DC: GPO, 1995.

Interviews

Anderson, Eric. Interview by author on 23 April 2006 at Ft Leavenworth, KS.

Anderson, Joseph. Interview by author on 23 April 2006 at Ft Leavenworth, KS.

Bookard, Joseph. Interview by author on 23 April 2006 at Ft Leavenworth, KS.

Giglione, Michael. Interview by author on 14 May 2006 at Ft Leavenworth, KS.

Flynn, Michael Flynn, Military Analyst, C2 Division, Combined Arms Doctrine Directorate. Interview by author on 26 May 2006, Ft Leavenworth, KS.

King, David. Interview by author on 23 April 2006 at Ft Leavenworth, KS.

Korando, Deitra. Interview by author on 23 April 2006 at Ft Leavenworth, KS.

London, David. Interview by author on 23 April 2006 at Ft Leavenworth, KS.

Pepper, Joseph. Interview by author on 23 April 2006 at Ft Leavenworth, KS.

Phelps, Christopher. Interview by author on 23 April 2006 at Ft Leavenworth, KS.

Internet Sources

Bhatia,Umej. "In the Shade of Death: A Critical Reading on Sayyid QutB's Qur'anic Exegesis." [article on-line]. Available from http://www.fsu.edu/~proghum/interculture/In%20the%20Shade%20of%20Death.htm. Internet. Accessed on 30 November 2005.

Bureau of Democracy. *Human Rights and Labor, International Religious Freedom Report*, U.S. Department of State. [report on-line]. Available from http://www.state.gov/g/drl/rls/irf/2004/35335.htm. Internet. Accessed on 16 January 2006.

Byrne, Edmund F. Mission in Modern Life: A Public Role for Religious Beliefs. Available from http://www.bu.edu/wcp/Papers/Poli/PoliByrn.htm. Internet. Accessed on 20 September 2005.

Chossudovsky, Michel. *The KLA: A Mystery Wrapped in an Enigma*, 1999. Available from http://www.antiwar.com/kla.html. Internet. Accessed on 23 November 2005.

Council on Foreign Relations. IRA Splinter Groups, 2005. Available from http://cfrterrorism.org/groups/realira.html. Internet. Accessed on 16 January 2006.

_____.. Northern Ireland Loyalist Paramilitaries. Available from http://cfrterrorism.org/groups/realira.html. Internet. Accessed on 16 January 2006.

Freeh, Louis J., Director, Federal Bureau of Investigation. Testimony before the United States Senate Committee on Appropriations, Armed Services, and Select Committee on Intelligence, 10 May 2001, "Threat of Terrorism to the United States." Available from http://www.fbi.gov/congress/congress01/freeh051001.htm. Internet. Accessed on 23 May 2006.

Hancock, Landon. "Northern Ireland: Troubles Brewing." Thesis, Institute for Conflict Analysis and Resolution, George Mason University, 1998. [thesis on-line]. Available from http://cain.ulst.ac.uk/othelem/landon.htm. Internet. Accessed on 2 December 2005.

Howard, Glenn E. *Unmasking Terror: A Global Review of Terrorist Activities* [book on-line]. Washington, DC: Brookings Institute and the Jamestown Foundation, 2005. Available from http://brookings.edu/unmaskingterror. Internet. Accessed on 3 January 2006.

Kennedy, Roger. The Battle of the Boyne, A paper presented to the New York Military Affairs Symposium, CUNT Graduate Center, 11 June 2004. Available from http://libraryautomation.com/nymas/boyne.html. Internet. Accessed on 28 November 2005.

Kohler, Peter. *Urban Legends and Folklore*. Available from http://ancienthistory. about.com/cs/grecoromanmyth1/a/whatismyth.htm. Internet. Accessed on 15 May 2005.

Kusovac, Zoran. "The KLA: Braced to Defend and Control." *Jane's Intelligence Review* (1999) [journal on-line]. Available from http://www.janes.com/defence/ news/kosovo/jir990401_01_n.shtml. Internet. Accessed on 25 November 2005.

Milosevic, Slobodan. Speech of Slobodan Milosevic at Kosovo Polje, translated by Tim Skorick, 24-25 April 1987. Available from http://www.slobodan-milosevic. org/news/milosevic-1987-3-eng.htm. Internet. Accessed on 18 November 2005.

MOUT. Lessons Learned Northern Ireland. Operational Lesson Learned 1. Available from http://www.geocities.com/Pentagon/6453/nireland.html. Internet. Accessed on 15 May 2006.

_____. Operational Lesson Learned 6. Available from http://www.geocities.com/ Pentagon/6453/nireland.html. Internet. Accessed on 15 May 2006.

_____. Tactical Lesson Learned 6. Available from http://www.geocities.com/ Pentagon/6453/nireland.html. Internet. Accessed on 15 May 2006.

Pike, John. Federation of American Scientist, Intelligence Resource Services. Serb Volunteer Guard [SDG / SSJ] "Arkan's Tigers;" 1 February 2000. Available from http://www.fas.org/irp/world/para/sdg.htm. Internet. Accessed on 30 November 2005.

_____. Federation of American Scientist, Intelligence Resource Services, *White Eagles Serbian Radical Party*, 3 October 1998. Available from http://fas.org/irp/ world/para/white_eagles.htm. Internet. Accessed on 30 November 2005.

President of the United States. *A Record of Achievement, Ratification of the Fifteenth Amendment*, 30 March 1870 [document on-line]. Available from http://www.grantstomb.org/civ/ exhciva.html. Internet. Accessed on 12 May 2006.

Public Broadcast System. Frontline: "Ambush in Mogadishu." [Article on-line] Available from http://www.pbs.org/wgbh/pages/frontline/shows/ambush/etc/cron.html. Internet. Accessed on 18 May 2006.

Rabasa, Angel M., Cheryl Benard, Peter Chalk, C. Christine Fair, Theodore Karasik, Rollie Lal, Ian Lesser, and David Thaler. *The Muslim World After 9/11*. Santa Monica, CA: RAND Corporation, 2004. Available from http://www.rand.org/ publications/RB/RB151/. Internet. Accessed on 20 November 2005.

Religious Tolerance.org. Religious Aspect of the Yugoslavia Kosovo Conflict, Catholic Peace Group Calls for Prompt Action to Avert Wider Conflict in Kosovo, 20 May

1998. Available from http://www.religioustolerance.org/war_koso.htm. Internet. Accessed on 20 November 2005.

Sells,Michael. "Christoslavism 2/The Five Major Components." 1996. Available from http://www.haverford.edu/relg/sells/postings/christoslavism2.html. Internet. Accessed on 30 November 2005.

Sii arag, A. Duale. "The Birth and Rise of Al-Ittihad Al-Islami in the Somali Inhabited Regions in the Horn of Africa." 13 November 2005. [Article on-line]. Available from http://www. wardheernews.com/articles/. Internet. Accessed on 2 December 2005

Southern Poverty Law Center. A Hundred Years of Terror, [report on-line]. Available from http://www. iupui.edu/~aao/kkk.html. Internet. Accessed on 16 January 2006.

"Three Levels of War" [article on-line]. Available from http://www.cadre.maxwell.af. mil/ar/MENTOR/vol1/sec02.pdf#search='%E2%80%9CEach%20level%20is%20 concerned%20with%20planning%20%28making%20strategy%29%2C. Internet. Accessed on 23 March 2006.

The Holy Bible. The First Scofield Study Bible, Ephesians 6:5-8. ed. C.I. Scofield. Belgium: World Bible Publishers, Inc., 1986.

The Molossian Military Academy, Homepage. Available from http://www.molossia. org/milacademy/strategy.html. Internet. Accessed on 23 March 2006.

Trondsen, Leif E. "Ol' Satan's Church is Here Below: Southern Religion and Black Slavery in the Antebellum South." [article on-line]. Available from http://www. anglocatholicsocialism.org/slavery.html. Internet. Accessed on 3 January 2006.

United Nations. The International Criminal Tribunal for the Former Yugoslavia, Case No. IT-99-37, The Prosecutor of the Tribunal against Slobodan Milosevic. Available from http://www.un.org/icty/indictment/english/mil-ii990524e.htm. Internet. Accessed on 28 November 2005.

US Commission on Internation Religious Freedom. Annual Report of the United Stated Commission on International Religious Freedom, May 2005. Available from http://www.uscirf.gov/countries/publications/currentreport/2005annualRpt.pdf. Internet. Accessed on 16 January 2006.

US State Department. 2002. Available from http://www.state.gov/g/drl/rls/irf/2001/ index.cfm?docid=553. Internet. Accessed on 27 September 2005.

Waal Alex. *Islamism and Its Enemies in the Horn of Africa*. Indianapolis, IN: University Press, 2004.

Webster's Ninth New Collegiate Dictionary. Spring Field, MA: Merriam-Webster Inc., 1990

Wikipedia. Juche. [Encyclopedia on-line]. Available from http://en.wikipedia. org/wiki/Juche. Internet. Accessed on 27 September 2005.

Ziv, Ilan. *Yellow Wasps: Anatomy of War Crimes*. Available from http://www.frif.com/ cat97/t-z/yellow_w.html. Internet. Accessed on 30 November 2005.